# THE MAKING OF HUDDERSFIELD

# The Making of
# Huddersfield

## George Redmonds

*Series Editor*
**Brian Elliott**

**Wharncliffe Books**

First published in Great Britain in 2003
and reprinted in 2009 and 2015 by
WHARNCLIFFE BOOKS
An imprint of
Pen & Sword Books Ltd
47 Church Street
Barnsley, South Yorkshire
S70 2AS

ISBN 978 1 90342 539 8

A CIP catalogue record for this book is
available from the British Library

Printed and bound in England
By CPI Group (UK) Ltd, Croydon, CR0 4YY

Pen & Sword Books Ltd incorporates the Imprints of Aviation, Atlas,
Family History, Fiction, Maritime, Military, Discovery, Politics, History,
Archaeology, Select, Wharncliffe Local History, Wharncliffe True Crime,
Military Classics, Wharncliffe Transport, Leo Cooper, The Praetorian Press,
Remember When, Seaforth Publishing and Frontline Publishing.

For a complete list of Pen & Sword titles please contact
PEN & SWORD BOOKS LIMITED
47 Church Street, Barnsley, South Yorkshire, S70 2AS, England
E-mail: enquiries@pen-and-sword.co.uk
Website: www.pen-and-sword.co.uk

# Contents

# $\mathcal{P}$REFACE

T*he Making of Huddersfield* is not a conventional history of the town. When Huddersfield celebrated one hundred years of borough status in 1968, it was then thought that its essential history might be captured in a single volume, continuing a tradition that had begun with Hobkirk and Sykes. Since then a wide range of articles, monographs and books has been published, drawing on much new source material and employing a much more integrated approach. So many new areas of interest have been opened up, and fresh light has been thrown on so many major past events, that it would be difficult now to envisage a town history that did not require several volumes.

The aim of *The Making of Huddersfield* is, therefore, to highlight certain aspects of the town's development by concentrating on the particular rather than the general; not to write a chronological overview of centuries of growth, but to select subjects that will best illustrate what was happening at different times, and deal with them in detail; more a series of illuminating snapshots than an all-embracing documentary. The historian's source materials are often hidden from view but here an attempt will be made to integrate them into the text, so that the reader might capture the excitement that original maps and documents can stimulate. Place-names too have an important role: they are one of the tools at the historian's disposal and they will be used here, not just for their etymologies, but to draw attention to important aspects of the town's history.

At the heart of the book will be the stories of people and families who played their part in the making of the town, but it will not be a catalogue of the achievements of the Ramsdens, as Lords of the Manor, nor an account of the local gentry as a whole, although these topics will be touched upon, but an insight into ordinary tenants such as the Appleyards and Dysons; a nineteenth century entrepreneur like James Stott; the property developer Lewis Fenton; Rene Trippier, an early refugee from France, and Thomas Haigh, a beleaguered mill-owner. It will be seen how certain families, such as the Brooks and the Hirsts, were at the heart of the town's expansion and how individuals could establish settlements that are now major areas of growth.

I should like to think that the book has several layers, starting with the landscape and the changes to it, both natural and man-made. Important background elements will be the fickle course of the River Colne, the drawing of boundaries and the status of communities: the clearance of scrub and trees, the building of houses, inns, highways and bridges, even market growth and industrial development. These will be illustrated through the people involved, whether Celts, Anglians and Scandinavians, or farmers, tanners, clothiers, innkeepers and shop-owners. The de Lacys, Fountains Abbey and the Knights Hospitaller have all played a part in Huddersfield's transformation and their presence during that transformation should gradually emerge, but they too are part of the background. The essential story is of individuals and groups of individuals who helped to shape the modern town, within a national context of momentous historical events.

Many of the topics in this book have formed the subject of lectures to WEA classes and of articles published in the *Huddersfield Examiner* over the last twenty-five years, and I am pleased to have this opportunity to bring them up to date and to make some necessary corrections. Also included are a number of previously unpublished items which have emerged from my continuing work on Huddersfield's history in, for example, the records of Quarter Sessions, wills, court rolls, and title deeds scattered over a wide area, some as far afield as North America. In general I have attempted not to go over well-trodden ground and that may at times have affected the balance of the subject matter but for those who want a fuller picture there are numerous additional publications to consult. These include my own *Old Huddersfield: 1500-1800*, the more recent *Huddersfield, a most handsome town* (1992) and the essays and booklets of Edward Law on a wide variety of topics.

I am grateful to the *Huddersfield Examiner* and to Kirklees Cultural Services in particular for their generosity in allowing me to use photographs from their extensive collections and to the late Clifford Stephenson who bequeathed so many of his books and photographs to me, and to my friend and brother-in-law, Tony Burke for his help with the illustrations. Wharncliffe Books should also be credited for their continuing enterprise in the field of Yorkshire local history and I acknowledge here the help I have had in the editing process from Brian Elliott. All local historians receive valuable advice from friends and colleagues and I am aware of my debt over the years to correspondents, students and fellow researchers, not just for the items of information that they have so readily shared with me but for their unflagging interest in Huddersfield's history. They are too many to mention but I am grateful to them nonetheless. Finally, I wish to say thank you also to Ann-marie my wife: I am no expert in the use of a word processor and if she were not there to bail me out at regular intervals this book would never have been finished.

George Redmonds, 2003.

# 1 HUDDERSFIELD AND ITS ENVIRONS

In 1801 the population of Huddersfield was 7,268 but that was the figure for the township as a whole not just the town itself. Included in the total were the residents of numerous farms and hamlets scattered over a wide area, all of them significant in the making of Huddersfield. The town's growth and influence in the nineteenth century saw its boundaries extend into other parishes and also into neighbouring territories, so that it came to incorporate parts of Kirkheaton and Almondbury and became the focal point in a much wider area. It is this area that I have called Huddersfield and its environs.

## Huddersfield – a village

In Elizabeth's reign Huddersfield had some status as the location of the parish church but it was still only a village and most of the early evidence we have relates to individual properties and families. In fact the earliest map of Huddersfield dates from 1716 and we have very little documentary evidence touching on the town centre from before 1627, the year of the first surviving court roll. So, if we are to form an idea of what the town may have looked like in the 1500s, we are mostly dependent on the occasional details which survive in title deeds. For example, a lease of 1589, from John Armytage of Kirklees to the daughters of William Blackburn, contains one or two fascinating paragraphs describing a property near the church. It was called 'the owtshotte', a sort of penthouse, and was first mentioned in 1517.

*Huddersfield Market Cross, photographed before the restoration work on the Market Place.* G Redmonds

The strip of land on which this lean-to was built was tiny, just '16 ellnes in lenght' (sic) and 'foure foote in breadthe'. It lay right next to the churchyard, abutting on the 'towne gate', and next to it was a tenter croft and a parcel of land 'palid in and lyenge betwixte the Capitall Messuage and the towne gate'. Parts of this capital messuage, or 'firehowse' as it was also called, 'were builded upon the waste' near 'Smithiehill'. In fact this is the earliest reference we have to the town's main street, later to be renamed Kirkgate, and to 'Smithiehill', a name which has not survived. The picture is essentially one of a rural village street.[1]

A second lease, of 1606, between William Taylier, a clothier, and John Turner, a butcher, had to do with 'one shoppe' which formed part of the former's 'Mansion howse' in 'Northbarre'. This was probably a cloth-dressing shop and it was proposed to convert it into a dwelling house. There was a garden on the south side but access to the shop, 'sufficient for horse and man' was actually through a neighbour's garden. There was 'free libertie to fetch water att the drawe well att all tymes for the use of the howse'. Norbar, as it was more commonly spelt, was a narrow lane at the bottom end of the town, the only other 'street' that Huddersfield then possessed, and here too the setting is rural not urban.[2]

*The earliest map of Huddersfield dates from 1716. This reconstruction of the town centre, c.1580, is based on the available documentary and map evidence.* G Redmonds

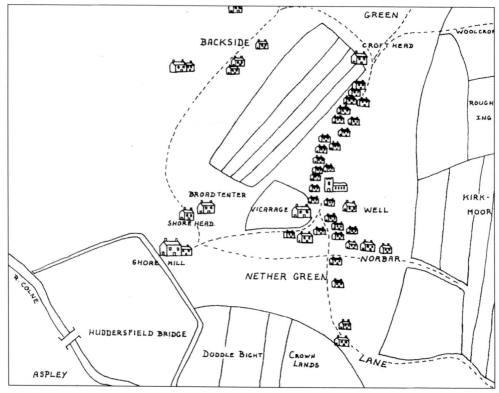

An even earlier deed records a grant of land in 1520 to John Hall, the vicar of Huddersfield. It was to be taken from the waste and its boundaries were defined as the vicar's newly constructed house, a field called 'Tenttar Croft', a lane called 'Huddersfeld layn' and 'Huddersfeld greyn' on the north.[3] We have already had a reference to Tenter Croft, close to the church, and these details make it clear that the land being granted was in the area later to be called Venn Street. They also confirm how undeveloped that central part of the town was in the early 1500s.

**The role of the Ramsdens**
The Ramsden family bought the manor of Huddersfield from Queen Elizabeth in 1599 and that of Almondbury in 1627, after which the two operated as a single estate. Although neither village was particularly large, much of the region's commercial activity must have focussed on Almondbury, which had been granted the right to hold markets and fairs in 1294. Huddersfield may in some respects have been better situated, but without a market it had little prospect of commercial development. The Ramsdens were eventually to change all that and establish Huddersfield as a major centre in the district, and there is a hint in the Calendar of State Papers that the idea may have been in their minds as early as 1632.

It was in July of that year that Sir John Ramsden, and his neighbour John Kaye of Woodsome, wrote to the authorities about the state of the retail trade in tobacco in the West Riding, and it seems that they already saw Huddersfield as a place of potential importance:

> *Having informed ourselves in what townes and places in Agbrigg within the West Riding Tobacco maye bee moste conveniently rentted and sould by Retaile wee have written to the chiefe officers and governers in Wakefield, Almondbury and Huddersfield (which townes we thinke fittest for that purpose) whoe have made certificate to us of their doeing and the same wee have sent forthwith to be presented to your Honnor.*

In the view of John Hirst and Edward Cowper the most suitable dealer in Huddersfield was a certain John Stasye who stocked 'sufficient for our whole township because there is so little tobacco used'. The fact that Almondbury had three retailers is a reflection on its traditional status but the reference to Huddersfield as a 'convenient' place for the trade and its inclusion alongside Wakefield and Almondbury is interesting.[4]

*The Market Charter of 1671, granted by Charles II to John Ramsden. It is displayed here by a member of the Huddersfield Library staff.* Courtesy of Kirklees Cultural Services

### The Market Charter

The Market Charter of 1671 granted the Ramsdens, as Lords of the Manor of Huddersfield, the right to hold a weekly market there on Tuesdays, for 'the buying and selling of all sorts of Cattle, Goods and Merchandise'. There is no doubt that this new-found status contributed considerably to the growth of the town and the story of Longroyd Bridge will later emphasise that point. We already know a great deal about the Market Place itself for the town is fortunate to have a run of estate maps from 1716 which show exactly where the market areas were. Now we can capture something of the flavour of a market day in Huddersfield from extracts taken from the records of the Quarter Sessions.

A case in 1728 concerns an alleged theft by Adam Dyson of South Crosland, but it is the testimony of Joshua Cuttell of Holmfirth that captures our attention. He stated that he had been:

> *...imploy'd by Abraham Roberts to sell a Piece of Plain Cloth at Huddersfield Market and not meeting with a Chapman for the same he laid it in a Closet in the house of Joseph Sikes, Innkeeper, and during the time that he went into the Market again... the cloth was stol'n.* [5]

The picture we have here is of clothiers seeking out prospective buyers as they moved between the market stalls and the ale-houses

*The King's Head Yard, Cloth Hall Street, c.1923. It was here that fancy manufacturers from Almondbury, Lepton, Honley and elsewhere formerly carried on their business.* G Redmonds sketch from a watercolour by C M Bishop

close by which offered them refreshment and overnight accommodation. It is easy to understand how such inns later became places where deals were struck and eventually the main centres of commercial activity.

There is no doubt that many who attended the market were obliged to spend a night in the town, either because they preferred not to ride home in the dark or because, as in the case of a Kirkburton butcher called John Smith (1715), they had been 'hindred from going home by bad weather'. The evidence reveals that John Smith 'being in the house of Edmond Shaw, Innkeeper, fell asleep on a Long Setle by the fire and whilst he was a sleep had about 40s taken out of his pocket'. The defendant Edward Archer was one of three clothiers said to have come 'forcibly into Edmond Shaw's house about one a Clock in the night time' and to have been 'very bussie about the said John Smith'.[6]

This case reminds us that there were no banks in the town until the nineteenth century, and that market traders would have had to carry their money about with them. This emerges in an earlier case of alleged theft (1706) in which the depositions capture another ordinary and yet revealing moment of Huddersfield life. The informant on this occasion was a Honley yeoman called Joseph Haigh, who described going into John Johnson's ale-house 'betwixt 8 and 9 of the clock in the morning... Calling for somebody to pull of his coat'. He must have risen early and ridden into town, stabling his horse before entering, for a servant woman called Elizabeth Cliff testified that she responded to his call and then 'took away his Coat and Whip'. According to Haigh he then pulled 'out of his pockett a bag of money in which was two and thirty pounds in silver', and bade Elizabeth Cliff 'take care of it and lay it by, it being his constant custom upon Market days... to committ his money... to the charge of some one of the Servants of John Johnson'. Later, when he asked the servant to fetch the money she denied that he had ever given it to her![7]

There were so many ale-houses round the Market Place and down the Town Street – today's Kirkgate – that it would not be surprising if some of the clothiers used market day as an excuse for noisy late-night drinking. No doubt drunkenness and crime went hand in hand, and in 1720 several labourers were arrested at Nathan Townend's house during a drinking session. It emerged in court that they had broken into the house of John Horsfall and stolen from his cellar 'fifty gallons of ale and beer and several pieces of beef and bread, valued at 40s'.[8]

*The Market Place with the* George Inn *in the background, c.1790. From a sketch by Fountain whose illustrations appear in H Morehouse's* History of Kirkburton, *1861.* Courtesy of Kirklees Cultural Services

One or two depositions relate to theft from the market stalls and one of the most picturesque concerned Nicholas Bramhall, described on this occasion in 1716 as a butcher, although he was possibly also an ale-house keeper and occasionally held the office of town constable. He claimed to have had 'a hinder quarter of Mutton and about seven or eight poundes of Sheep's Sewet taken out of his shop or stand in the market place', by Elizabeth Armitage. It is this woman's confession which allows us to picture Bramhall's stall, for she admitted that 'she took the Mutton off three crooks (i.e. hooks) and the Sewet she found upon a Clogg'. The 'clogg' was no doubt the thick wooden block traditional on a butcher's premises.[9]

Two other incidents record customs associated with the recovery of stolen property. The first took place on Fair Day, 4 May 1717, and concerned 'a piece of Druget', a coarse woollen material used as a floor covering. This had been found in the possession of a young Irish boy, John Wilson of Drogheda, seen with it 'near Huddersfield town end' by William Chadwick, and it was reclaimed by William Kay who 'own'd it to be his... seeing Michael Bell, servant to James Murgatroyd, constable, crying (it) about town'.[10] To 'own' was the term commonly used in the sense of 'claim' or 'recognise' and it occurred again in 1719, although on this occasion the stolen property was 'old pewter'. Hannah Robinson of Halifax told how a certain Sarah Blackburn had 'brought several pieces... to her husband's stall to exchange for new', but she was suspicious and informed James Whitekar, who 'came and owned two pewter pints and a salt'.[11]

Market day was customarily the day when miscreants were punished, either by being exposed on the pillory, their crime written on a piece of paper and pinned to their clothing, or by being whipped until they bled. In such cases the unfortunate person was fastened to the tail of a cart in front of one of the town's main inns and flogged all the way down to the corn mill at Shorefoot. Susannah Berry, for example, a widow found guilty in 1729 of felony, was first whipped at Wakefield and then at Huddersfield on the following market day, 'betwixt the hours of 12 and 1 o clock of the same day, from Michael Bramhall's house down to the Mills'.[12] An offender in 1745 was 'whipt from the *George* to the mill'.[13]

*A view of Kirkgate from the church, late 1800s.* Courtesy of Kirklees Cultural Services

James Murgatroyd, who was the landlord of the *George*, figured prominently in the town's affairs, whether as constable or innkeeper, victim or transgressor. In 1718, for instance, a goose was stolen out of his back garden by Thomas Whittell and Thomas Lockwood junior. The theft was discovered by William Child who in the early hours 'betwixt one and two a clock, hearing the dogs bark... went out to see what was the matter and looking over the Church-yard wall saw two men... but could not tell what they were doing'. He heard the men talking, one of them saying to the other 'wrap her up' and so, as they went 'down the Church yard he met them at the Church gates – one of them proving to be Thomas Whittell, who had a Goose under his arm'. This man's companion later testified that he and Whittell had been 'going down the Street together, having a Mastiffe bitch along with them...(which) seized of a goose'.[14]

On another occasion, in 1726, Murgatroyd told the magistrates how he had had fourteen deal boards taken out of his backyard and that he suspected two local carpenters, Joseph Drake and Richard Boothroyd. It is their confession which again emphasises the semi-rural nature of Huddersfield at that time, for Drake told how he had carried some of the boards into William Stacy's nearby barn and others into the Bone Crofts – the fields which lay directly to the south of the town's main street.[15] Of course, the *George* then occupied a prominent site in the town street and, as the most prestigious of the town's inns, may have been an obvious target for thieves. On the other hand James Murgatroyd may have been the sort of landlord who attracted enemies, for on at least three occasions he was brought before the magistrates accused of assault. One of these was an affray involving twelve men in which clubs, knives and swords were used but other, more personal, attacks were on John Armitage and his immediate neighbour Christopher Hebden, a 'gentleman'.

An earlier case, in 1679, offers another picture of Huddersfield as a 'village'. According to Abraham Sykes he was drinking with Richard Standidge in James Swallow's ale-house when Richard suggested to him and Thomas Brook that they should 'goe and knock downe two or three duckes, being then in Huddersfield Street'. The suggestion was taken up and the two men, 'did forthwith goe and kill four or five of the Ducks' and handed them over to Standidge and his wife Sarah.[16] In such cases we seldom have all the facts but the fragments that survive help us to imagine what the town was once like.

### The Pig Market

The story of Huddersfield's markets and fairs has already been well told by Edward Law, and he noted that the Pig Market was referred to as a separate market in a rental of 1836. It was then part of the holding of Joseph Kaye, a man who had a number of business interests and was already supplying pigs to the infirmary in 1833. On maps it was usually called the Swine Market and lay to the south of the shambles, where Victoria Street was.[17] We are fortunate to have an eye witness account by Sir George Head of how the pigs were prepared for sale on market day, after their long journey on foot over the Pennines from Liverpool. It seems that the market had achieved a certain amount of celebrity, sufficient to capture Sir George's attention:

> *On arriving at the market place half an hour before the time of commencing business, not a pig was to be seen; but on learning that the different droves were at that time undergoing ablution at the river, I walked thither in order to see the performance. Few indeed are the services a pig receives at the hands of his master without remonstrance... on the present occasion, to my great surprise, for I should have thought washing second only to shearing, every pig submitted to the ceremony with most perfect complacency; in fact, being heated and feverish after their journey they seemed delighted by the cooling process. The herd being driven up to their bellies in the river one man was entirely occupied in sluicing them with water from a pail, which he continually dipped in the stream and emptied over their backs. Another fellow anointed them one after another with yellow soap and so soon as he had raised a copious lather rubbed the hide first soundly with his hands and then with the teeth of a horse-mane comb. Now and then, in particular cases, it became necessary to have recourse to an instrument of still greater power, his broad thumb nail. After rubbing and lathering for some time they were sluiced again, and as pailful after pailful descended on their hides, no sound was heard among them – not even a wince or snort; on the contrary, every now and then a soft, happy grunt... seemed unequivocally to describe their perfect content and satisfaction.*[18]

In the early nineteenth century the road that ran from the bottom of Kirkgate to Shorehead was called Low Green Road but, as the town became more conscious of its status, this was changed to Castle Street and then Castlegate. According to John Hanson, who wrote about the town in 1878,[19] it acquired this name from the town lock-up, known locally as Towser Castle because the town constable's dog had the name Towser. That seems unlikely to be true as there were

*The top side of Castlegate, looking towards Leeds Road, 1930.* Courtesy of Kirklees Cultural Services

towers in other northern towns, but at least it suggests that there was a lock-up from *c.*1800. Now there is evidence that it may have been in place much longer, possibly from *c.*1730 in response to an order from the magistrates. It was at the Quarter Sessions, in 1728, that the Huddersfield constable reported to the court that the town was 'very much infested and oppressed with vagrants and strollers', so much so that he had been obliged to 'charge persons to his aid in secureing them'. He said the town needed 'a kidd coat or prison' and twenty-nine local people signed his petition, most of them identifiable as important members of the community. The list included Alexander Macauley, Francis Watts, Nicholas Bramhall, William Stacy and Marmaduke Hebden.[20] 'Kidcote' was the old word in Yorkshire for a lock-up and the one formerly on Ouse Bridge in York features in documents from the early 1400s.

**Estate records – the late 1700s**

Sir John Ramsden, the fourth Baronet and the ninth generation of the family in Huddersfield, was born in 1755 and inherited the estate fourteen years later. He died in 1839, having outlived his son, and during his stewardship of the manor he steered the town through momentous years of change. His father had met the challenge of the 1760s by providing Huddersfield with a Cloth Hall and his grandson was to develop the north end of the town, bringing it into the Railway Age. Sir John, though, will always be remembered as the Ramsden who financed the construction of the canals and thereby revolutionised communications between Huddersfield and its potential markets.

The Ramsden story is a fascinating one and much of it has already been well told. What is seldom realised is that the details of the story are in the family's papers in Kirklees archives, in the apparently routine entries in deeds, court rolls, surveys and rentals. From the Middle Ages to the present day the pages of Huddersfield's history are there to be turned by amateur and professional alike.

Particularly valuable are the various surveys of the town that were carried out for the Ramsdens once they held the lordship of the manor, for they provide information on all manner of topics.[21] For example, the survey and map of 1778 demonstrate how important Huddersfield's public houses had become in the century following the market charter. In those days the line of the main street, today's Kirkgate and Westgate, was the major axis of the town and there was no street running north and south on the line of modern New Street and John William Street. In fact where John William Street now begins was the *George* which dates from 1687 at least and is probably the town's oldest hostelry. It may have dominated the north side of the market square but it was only one of many public houses there. On the east were the *White Boar*, the *Brown Cow* and the *King's Arms*, and on the south the *Horse and Jockey*. All these had stabling to the rear and at least two had their own brew-house. On the west side of the square was the impressive *Queen's Head*, the buildings grouped round a courtyard.

There were many other inns and beer houses east and west of the square, a total altogether of twenty-four or twenty-five, and most of these appear to have been built after the granting of the market charter. Particularly prominent was the *Swan*, in its present position but with stabling across the way, along what is now Byram Street. It was about this time that New Street was begun and the first buildings are shown on the map, defining a new direction for traffic and

*Huddersfield Cloth Hall. It opened in 1766 and was demolished in 1930.* Courtesy of the *Huddersfield Examiner*

*The 'New or Brick Buildings' in New Street, completed in the 1790s.* G Redmonds

commercial activity. Ironically, that area is now a pedestrian area along with its southern extension, and the old name Buxton Road is almost forgotten. 'Buxton' signalled clearly the direction in which the road was heading, and it dates back to the building of the Huddersfield to Woodhead turnpike of 1768-69.

Another document with a story to tell is the rent book of 1798, meticulously kept by Sir John Ramsden's agent. Looked at from one point of view it tells us in simple arithmetical terms where the money came from that financed the great enterprises – from the modest rents of a few shillings to the enormous sum of £445 that William Bradley paid for his collieries, his tolls and the *Bull's Head* tavern. The landlord of the *George Inn*, from which the present *George Hotel* takes its name, paid £315 rent, while Abraham Beaumont at the *Pack Horse* paid £80. But it was not just house rents and public houses that brought in the money: the rent for the *Shambles* was £67 11s; Mr Midwood's malt kiln was £27 10s and one sum of £210 was received from Richard Clay 'on account of navigation' – the canal beginning to pay its way.

There was also Mr Stanton's theatre, William Charter's market gardens, collieries, quarries and brick works, all contributing to a large income. But the expense of running the estate was also large and the story of how some of the money was spent is no less interesting. There were bills, inevitably, for repairs to property, for making fences, sinking wells and building barns. There were staff wages which now sound incredibly modest; Joseph Brook received 4s 2d as 'a year's salary for overlooking woods', while 10s went to the Almondbury schoolmaster for six months' service. Other larger sums paid the vicar's land tax or went to the Duke of Leeds and the Governors of Clitheroe School – each payment a story in itself.

Progress came at a price. Collieries had to be inspected and surveyed, and expert advice sought on a variety of engineering projects; 'to Mr Heywood for his opinions on sundry matters as to Huddersfield canal, 2 guineas'. Even the very small payments can be of interest; the 'postage of letters and carriage of parcels' accounted for nearly £3, which may not sound very much – unless we compare it with Joseph Brook's annual salary. And there was also the traditional tenants' meal, paid for by the landlord, and enjoyed, no doubt, by the '252 men and 69 women'.

There are other ways of course in which such a document can be used to throw light on the town, and the surnames of the tenants themselves are a vital genealogical source, especially when studied in a sequence of rentals. In a similar way we can use the information on

*The Pack Horse yard in the early 1900s.* Clifford Stephenson

place-names, for the usual works of reference often take the so-called minor names no further back than the first Ordnance Survey maps or the tithe award of 1851. This rental can, therefore, help us build up the history of the major farms and hamlets, and also such apparently insignificant places as Jockey Hall, Crooked Tree, Engine Bridge, Sally Carr, Norbar and Squirrel Ditch, fascinating names that remain obscure or have long since disappeared.

## The Pinfold

The pinfold was the place where animals that had strayed were kept until the owner reclaimed them, on payment of a fine. Locally they were built on common land; small round enclosures, made of stone and with a low doorway, and several of them survive in the area in reasonably good repair, notably those at Slaithwaite, Crosland and Scammonden. The Farnley Tyas pinfold lies at the side of Hey Lane but very few of its stones are still standing, whilst in Lepton nothing remains but the place-name Pinfold Lane. Huddersfield's pinfold seems to have totally escaped the attention of local historians and yet it once featured in several minor court cases.

The earliest of these was in 1687 when three men, William Standidge, Walter Butler and Henry Crowther, complained that their horses, which had been grazing quite legally on the verges of Huddersfield Lane, had been removed by Richard Chadwick, the pinder. The men suspected that he was abusing his authority and took 'an oppertunaty to watch the horses and did see the pinder take them out of the lanes... and drive them to the Common pound'. Chadwick demanded twenty shillings for their release, 'pretending that the horses had been trespassers' and when that was refused took the animals to Almondbury pinfold, presumably to thwart any attempt by the owners to rescue them. George Mitchell made a similar complaint and the pinder was finally indicted at the Quarter Sessions.[22]

On another occasion, in 1738, David Hepworth reported that he had 'distrained' five cows in Deighton 'for divers trespasses' committed by John Brook and William Mitchell. As he was driving the cows 'to the common pinfold' he was waylaid by the two men who 'rescued' the animals and drove them away.[23] Not surprisingly Huddersfield's pinfold did not survive the town's development but at least we know exactly where it stood. It is shown on George Crosland's map of 1826 at a point we can now identify as the junction of Back Union Street and Leeds Road.

**The Commercial**

Every public house has its own history, but the growing importance of the area from New Street to High Street, from the early 1800s, is reflected in the story of the aptly named *Commercial*. In recent years more than one well-established town centre public house has changed its name, presumably in the hope of persuading people that a new name signals a better future. This desire for something that was catchy and modern saw the *Commercial* become the *Jug and Bottle* and it was particularly popular for a time among young people. It has continued to thrive since the old name was restored and for those who love tradition it is good to see this bit of old Huddersfield restored. The inn stands at the junction of High Street and New Street and it consists of two buildings of different height, both in vernacular style; the taller building fronts onto New Street and the other onto High Street. Until the recent alterations the corner part of

*The* Commercial, *High Street, in the 1980s. The corner site was still occupied by Preedys, the tobacconists.* G Redmonds

the complex was traditionally a tobacconist's and this too is part of the history of the *Commercial*.

It is a history which begins in the early 1800s, for before that the corner site was occupied by a barn and stackyard – possibly the very barn described by John Hanson when he wrote of his boyhood in *c*.1800 and recalled how he had played in a High Street barn, trampling on 'the fragrant hay in the old loft, time-blackened and cobweb-hung'.[24] There were still green fields in New Street then, and High Street, despite its name, was no busy thoroughfare, merely a track along the old Back Green, with a few new buildings announcing its aspirations. One of those buildings, in the years prior to 1822, was a shop selling tea, flour and other groceries – probably the lower building which still fronts onto High Street. It was run by a man with the unusual name Anby Beatson who was granted a publican's licence at the Brewster Sessions in 1828. Actually his tenancy since 1815 had been linked with that of John and James Milnes, who were brewers and had premises looking on to New Street, so it is possible that beer had already been sold there for some time.

From the 1830s the public house is listed in trade directories as the *Commercial* and this makes it easier to trace the landlords. Anby Beatson was followed by John Gill, Benjamin Ainley, Benjamin Hutchinson and Joshua Lee, but little is known about any of these men, and the only point of interest concerns Benjamin Ainley. He became landlord in 1847, probably moving there from the *Druids Hotel* in Temple Street which was demolished to make way for the new railway station. It has been said that it was later re-erected as the *Zetland*.

A detailed insurance map, drawn in 1887 when Joshua Lee was the landlord, gives us a clear idea of the lay-out of the premises and the function of each building.[25] It shows that the *Commercial* was at 62 New Street and that the corner shop was kept by Benjamin Wade, a tobacconist. His immediate neighbour in High Street was Henry Scott, a fruiterer, occupying the premises where Anby Beatson had first lived. The yard to the rear of all these premises was reached via a passage to the north of the *Commercial*, beyond which lay Young's Brush Factory.

The Youngs had been neighbours of the *Commercial* since 1830 at least, no doubt living above the shop. However, when Henry Tweed Young was running the business, *c*.1900, the family had their home at 3 Murray Road, Edgerton, and it may be that this move took place when the emphasis changed from retailing to manufacture. It is more difficult to decide just when the tobacconist's was established, but certainly Benjamin Wade was in business there from *c.*1880. The address of the *Commercial* had changed just before this, from 64 to 62 New Street, so the explanation behind what happened is likely to lie in the title deeds to the property.

Eventually, of course, the public house was to take over both the fruiterer's and the tobacconist's, and to change its name, but all this was a long way ahead, and those few people who can remember the Huddersfield of over eighty years ago will know that the businesses of Wade and Young still flanked the New Street frontage of the inn as the Great War broke out.

## Pollution

A title deed of 1808 provides us with a vivid picture of developing Huddersfield, highlighting some of the problems associated with industrial growth. It is a lease for a newly-erected building on a 'piece of ground... adjoining on Manchester Street' and there is an accompanying plan giving the exact dimensions and location, including some land marked out for additional premises. It is the next part of the deed that is most interesting for it specifies what the

*Granby Street, lying between Manchester Street and Upperhead Row, 1939.*
Courtesy of Kirklees Cultural Services

tenant was not allowed to do, and that included exercising the 'trade of a Blacksmith, Farrier, Tanner, Skinner or Chymist', or using the building 'as a Slaughter House, or a place for making Pots or Tobacco pipes, Burning of blood, making of Glue or Sizing, Soap or Candles – or any other noisome or dangerous calling'. Nor might the premises 'be used for a shop or stall for vending or exposing to sale any broad or narrow, undressed woollen cloths, coatings or shalloons... or any Flesh or Butchers Meat on any Market Day'. The tenant was also required to 'pave with Boulder or other stones and repair and maintain such parts of the said streets called Manchester Street and Upperhead Row as is contained from the crown or centre thereof'. A link with Huddersfield's medieval past is contained in the clause that obliged the tenant to 'grind all his corn and malt at the Corn Mills of Sir John Ramsden'.[26]

## A self-made man
Some thirty or so years ago developments in the centre of Huddersfield, and the creation of new motorway links, brought about the demolition of two old buildings, neither perhaps with any great claim to fame or beauty, but which together served to remind us of a man whose life story epitomised the business sense and enterprise of

*Haigh Cross, Lindley Moor, now situated behind the farmhouse but formerly at the road junction.* Tony Burke

*The Viaduct, Huddersfield, from St John's Road, 1907.* Clifford Stephenson

nineteenth century Huddersfield. That man was James Stott and the first of the two buildings was the three-storey warehouse known as Stott's Buildings, near to the site of the present fire station; the second was Woodlands House on Lindley Moor, demolished when the M62 was built. There is little now to tell us that an imposing Victorian villa once stood on that site.

There can be few people now alive who know anything at all about James Stott, for he died well over a century ago, and yet, from the facts available in local records, and with a little imagination, it is possible to reconstruct a life which is equally as fascinating as those of contemporaries who were pioneering the new overseas territories. It is a story which begins at Haigh Cross, high above the town on windswept Lindley Moor. The census returns show that James was living there in 1841, aged eighteen, with his father and two brothers, Lewis and David. His father, who was also called James, was a clothier, aged fifty-five – probably the J Stott who had discovered Roman coins at Haigh Cross in 1824. It is tempting to speculate just what sort of education young James Stott may have received and what connection there may have been between his family and that of Joseph Stott, who was a celebrated local historian in his day and lived nearby at Haigh House Hill.

Unfortunately, evidence for that is lacking but using the census returns we at least find out that James was a married man in 1851 with a daughter six years old. He was an 'engine tenter' – one of the new breed of proud mechanics who gave such impetus to the Industrial Revolution – and he had moved to Upperhead Row at the top end of the town. Nothing at this stage marks him out from scores of his contemporaries but Huddersfield was now part of the railway network, engaged in a new and vigorous phase of its development, and the estate rent books reveal that James Stott was alert to the possibilities.

The entries for 1852, for example, show that he had become a modest property owner, paying rent on six cottages and one shop, not to mention his own house at Swallow Street. He did this by using the Building Clubs which were based in local public houses, the forerunners of today's Permanent Building Societies. By the 1860s he was sufficiently well off to have established two town-centre businesses. According to the trade directories of 1866 and 1868 he still lived at Upperhead Row, but was carrying on a business in rags, bones, iron and salt at 11 Viaduct Street.

The circumstances of his second venture are less clear but he was described in the 1861 census as a master grocer and, in a near contemporary directory, as a master grocer and rag dealer. He operated both businesses throughout this period from his two addresses in Viaduct Street and Upperhead Row. It is here that oral evidence plays an important part, for Eric Armitage, the great grandson of James Stott, remembered being told that his ancestor had also kept an eating-house or dining rooms, where he catered for labourers engaged on local railway works. Perhaps this was an extension of the grocery side of his business.

Even more illuminating is the Burgess Roll of 1875. In it James is described as a marine-store dealer with a house and shop at 86 and 88 Upperhead Row and a Rag Merchant's business in Viaduct Street. But that is not all, for he was also in partnership with a man called Ashworth at New Mill in Stainland, manufacturing Press

Papers, Glazed Casing, etc. – all the details still listed on a trade card kept by Eric Armitage that is over one hundred years old. One can imagine James Stott, during the prosperous years of the 1870s, riding over to Stainland from his home in Upperhead Row and, as he passed Haigh Cross, thinking back to his boyhood. He was now in his fifties, a successful manufacturer, and it comes as no surprise to discover that some time before 1879 he moved to the fine Victorian house at Woodlands on Lindley Moor. James Stott had 'arrived'.

What followed this move is not clear. Mary Stott, his wife, died at Woodlands in 1879 but two years later James was still living there and carrying on his Stainland and Huddersfield businesses. He must however, have relinquished them soon afterwards and the trade directory of 1884 provides us with an amusing postscript. In it his home address is given as Woodthorpe not Woodlands, a subtle change that reflects his rise in status, whilst his occupation at Upperhead Row was that of Glass and China Dealer. His days as a Rag Merchant were truly over.

### A French immigrant

Sebastian Burluraux is an unlikely name to find in a nineteenth century Huddersfield trade directory, but there it is from the 1850s to the 1870s, at various addresses in Kirkgate. His advertisement for 1879 shows that he was dealing principally in basket ware, both as a retailer and wholesaler, and that some of the stock was being

*An advertisement in the* Huddersfield Directory *for 1879.* G. Redmonds collection

## S. BURLURAUX,

WHOLESALE & RETAIL FRENCH, ENGLISH & GERMAN

## BASKET ESTABLISHMENT,

### 10, KIRKGATE, HUDDERSFIELD.

S. B. begs most respectfully to thank the Gentry and Public of Huddersfield and Vicinity for past favours, and also to inform them that he now has a very large Stock of all kinds of BASKETS at very Reduced Prices. Also a large Stock of BRUSHES of all kinds; WOODEN ARTICLES of all sorts; and a large assortment of TOYS at very low Prices.

### CABINET GOODS IN GREAT VARIETY.

### *CANE SEATED CHAIRS RE-BOTTOMED.*

XLVI

*The* Swan *Yard, demolished in 1878. It extended along what is now Byram Street.*
Courtesy of Kirklees Cultural Services

imported from France and Germany. Other items up for sale were cabinet goods, brushes, toys and wooden articles of all kinds. The only hint that some basket work was done on the premises is in the offer to re-bottom cane-seated chairs.

The surname looks French but it is not listed in a dictionary of French surnames, so I was delighted to have the problem of Sebastian's origins cleared up for me by a correspondent.[27] It seems that he was born in northern France about 1833 and left for England in his late teens. In 1851, when he was eighteen, he was a lodger at 8 Swan Yard, close to his business premises in Kirkgate, but that whole range of buildings was later demolished to make way for Byram Street. The interesting thing is that at least four other members of the family also made their way to England at that time and set up related businesses in Leeds and Newcastle upon Tyne. They obviously remained in touch, for Sebastian was married in Leeds in 1854 and his eldest son married in Newcastle in 1881. It may even be that they were all part of a larger-scale migration, since there were other people employed in these businesses who were of French birth.

# $\mathscr{T}$HE TOWNSHIP OF MARSH

The named wastes and commons of Huddersfield manor formerly included Cowcliffe, Sheepridge and Marsh, the latter describing an area to the west of the present town. In the sixteenth century the process of enclosure and settlement was under way and very soon the families living there developed a strong enough sense of community to feel independent of Huddersfield, although administratively still part of it. That situation was formally acknowledged when Marsh became a hamlet or sub-division of the township, a status which it retained until comparatively recently. Even now, although much of the area has been built over, there is still a feeling that it has its own identity and is not exactly part of the town.

It is very difficult to say what the original extent of Marsh was, or even how old the place-name is. It certainly included what we now know as Paddock, first recorded in the sixteenth century, for in 1775 the north end of Longroyd Bridge was said at the Quarter Sessions to be 'situated in the Hamlet of Marsh'.[28] Moreover, if the name pre-dated Edgerton and Gledholt, which may originally have had hamlet status, then these ancient single-family settlements may actually have been the first encroachments on Marsh common.

Because of the location of Marsh, which formed a sort of no-man's land between the ancient townships of Huddersfield and Quarmby, there is a temptation to think that the word may originally have meant 'boundary', on the lines of the word 'march' that we are familiar with in the expression 'the Welsh Marches'. On the whole, however, the linguistic evidence seems to suggest that we should take the word at its face value and accept that it was called Marsh simply because parts of it were marshy.

Two of the earliest and most significant references to the locality seem to have escaped the attention of local historians. In 1436 a grant by the Beaumonts to William Couper, of Edgerton, gave him permission to establish new boundaries on his land. These were to be ditches and banks crowned with thorn hedges. In the words of the deed William Couper was 'to make a dyke and lay it with qwykwode'. These new boundaries extended 'from the hedge at the Marche on the west side', to the hedge 'by the east side of Snodenhyll'.[29] Few Huddersfield people would recognise the name Snodenhyll, even in its present form of Snodley, but the hill in question is where the former service reservoir was located, at the point where Mountjoy Road joins Trinity Street.

The second reference, in another Beaumont deed of 1519, lists 'Snodlee' mentioned above, along with 'Thorpefeldes' and Marsh Cross.[30] Thorpe Fields does not appear to have survived, but one possibility is that it referred to a farm on the site of Heaton Fold. There is no direct evidence for that, but a clothier called Roger Heaton who was said to be 'of Marsh', took a lease in 1611 on a house called Thorpe Hall, and this may have been re-named after him.[31] More interesting, perhaps, is the early mention of Marsh Cross. No trace of this survives, but it is drawn on the map of 1716 and gave its name to a farm in the Eldon Road area. In fact, an earlier name for Eldon Road was Cross Lane. The presence of a cross on such a site is typical in Huddersfield township and others were located at road junctions on the commons of Cowcliffe and Sheepridge. There are several surviving cross bases in the district, but few of them have attracted much attention.

### Early settlements on the Marsh

The first clear evidence of new settlements in the Marsh area is in sixteenth-century sources. In the enclosures of *c.*1580 two men, Edward Smith and Edmond Mallinson, both took one acre 'upon the marshe'[32] and both are referred to as residents there in the parish registers. Other surnames found in that part of Huddersfield before 1600 were Batley, Heaton, Brook and Gledhill, with Hirst and France recorded soon afterwards. The association of the Batleys with the area

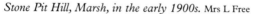
*Stone Pit Hill, Marsh, in the early 1900s.* Mrs L Free

*Greenhead Park was created out of an estate that had its origins in the Hirsts' tenancy of the early 1500s. It was saved from development in 1869 by Alderman Thomas Denham and formally opened in 1884.* G Redmonds collection

was to be a long one; in 1640 a John Batley of Marsh was named in the court rolls as the victim of an assault by William Taylor of Bay Hall, and in the estate rental of 1716 the two most prominent Marsh tenants were Joshua and William Batley. In the nineteenth century another William Batley 'of New North Road' acted as trustee for many of the early money clubs or Building Societies. Batley Street serves to remind us of that association.

To say that someone was 'of Marsh' was no longer adequate identification by the 1650s. The population was still not very large but there had been further encroachments and each of the scattered cottages had its own name in the parish records: Hirsts lived at the Cross, Horsfalls at Lathe, and Brooks at Tolson's and Coit. Most such place-names finally disappeared, probably as the once isolated cottages were absorbed into later housing developments, but there is a suggestion in the phrase 'the inhabitants of the marsh', first used in

*John Mellor's house in Paddock, 1863.* Courtesy of Kirklees Cultural Services

the court rolls in 1657, that Marsh was finally being thought of as a community. This status brought with it certain responsibilities, one of which was the maintenance of its own highways, and disputes about these confirm the locality's new-found sense of identity.

In a sequence of manorial bye-laws for 1657 the task of repairing the road from Huddersfield to Marsh was shared between the two places, with Marsh responsible for 'the highway leading from the house of John Hirst of the greene to the Marsh yate' – suggesting that Greenhead was then on the boundary between the two.[33] We can picture the 'yate' or gate in the fence that divided them. In 1692 Alice Hirst of Gledholt, a widow, felt aggrieved enough to complain to the magistrates at the Quarter Sessions that she was being taxed as a resident of Huddersfield and her petition is worth quoting in full for the light it throws on the problems arising from the new arrangement:

> *That youe would be pleased to grant the assistance of this Court against John Armitage and Robert Read of Huddersfield, overseers for the highways of the Toune only, who by their overpoureing would cause your pore Complainant to be asseased to the highways belonginge to the toune of Huddersfeild and She is a Inhabitant in a nother hamblitt whear She with the rest of the Inhabitantes belonginge that place called Marsh doth assist and to her proportion doth her part as may appear by one James Broadbent in this Court reddey to make it more fully appeare who humbly desireth he may be called to Speake.*

A number of events abut the turn of the century confirm the emergence of Marsh as a recognised sub-division of the township. In 1690, for example, the court rolls record the election of overseers for Marsh, along with those of Fartown, Deighton and Bradley. In October 1707, at Leeds Quarter Sessions, it was ordered that 'the severall Hamletts of Huddersfield' should 'for the future repair their highways separately', a matter which was agreed with 'the General Consent of the Inhabitants'. Marsh was one of the four hamlets named and the detailed rental of the Ramsdens' estate for 1716 confirms its independence, with a separate list of residents under the heading 'At the Marsh and Parrack', i.e. Paddock.[34] It was stated in 1741 that the inhabitants of Marsh had 'been accustomed to repair... the Highway from Paddock Foot to the bottom of Outcoat Bank', thus identifying the hamlet's eastern boundary with the town.[35]

**Developments at Blacker Lane**
Blacker Road, formerly known as Blacker Lane, was once part of the highway which ran from Longroyd Bridge to Jack Bridge in Birkby – a route which by-passed Huddersfield town centre and linked the Colne Valley directly with the old roads to Halifax, Bradford and Leeds. The origins of the ancient highway are unknown, but it may have started as a footway, giving access to and from the medieval settlements of Gledholt and Edgerton. It is certainly much older than the name Blacker Lane might suggest.

The Blackers were a prominent yeoman family, established in Worsbrough and then Crigglestone from the thirteenth century, and just what brought Richard Blacker to that part of Marsh has not been established. He was certainly living there in the 1580s and

In Loving Memory of
Our Dearest
JOSEFINE WLRCHOUNIG
DIED 7TH FEBRUARY 1964
AGED 42 YEARS.

was followed by his son William and then James, possibly his grandson. The court rolls show that Grace Blacker held 'land near Blackeryate' in 1631, along with James, but was the sole tenant in 1657, and she may have been the last of the line. Blackeryate must have referred to the 'yate' or gate which separated the family's cultivated land from Marsh common: these fields were called Blacker Crofts in 1677.[36]

The tenant that year was named as John Hirst which is one further clue to a direct connection between the Blackers and the Hirsts of Gledholt and Greenhead. In 1645, for example, a prominent captain in Sir John Savile's Troop of Horse, by the name of Ferdinand Blacker, wrote of a substantial sum of money which he had 'left att Widdowe Martha Hurst's in Greenhead'. It was one item in a document designed to put his financial affairs in order, for he was to fight a duel the day after and could not be sure of the outcome.[37] Despite the importance of the Hirsts in that part of the town it was the relatively short connection with the Blackers which gave the lane its name. The earliest reference to it is in the court roll of 1680, when the Marsh tenants were ordered to 'put one Lane called Blacker Lane into good repair'. It was then no more than a country track and it is hardly surprising that little is said about it in Huddersfield's records. The eighteenth century accounts of Fartown's surveyors of the highways refer to repair work carried out at their end of the lane, and it was defined in the *Huddersfield Enclosure Act* in 1789, but more detailed references occur only when it had come under threat of development. Perhaps the first major change came with the building of the Turnpike Road to Halifax and the erection of the Edgerton bar-house, for this severed Blacker Lane and was eventually responsible for the re-naming of the southern section. However, the northern section skirted Mr Lewis Fenton's property, and his decisions were to have a much more dramatic impact on the landscape.

A map of his estate in 1857 shows the land to the east of the lane set aside for the new Highfield cemetery, and that to the west marked out for building. The new streets cut through fields and woodland, in bold curving lines, and the area was described in Mr Fenton's accounts as 'eligible as building ground for the erection of first class villas' – today's Queen's Road and Murray Road. The locality was said to be 'the most attractive in the neighbourhood – the nearest property to Huddersfield on which satisfactory leases might be granted' and it was extremely popular with the public. The cemetery was laid out and the houses built, anticipating the larger-scale

*Blacker Road from Highfield Cemetery, 1996.*
Courtesy of the *Huddersfield Examiner*

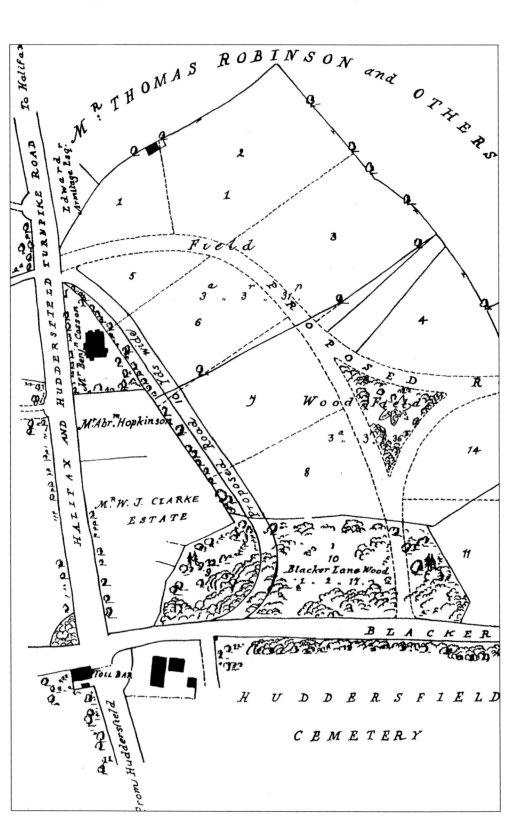

*A section of the map of 1857 which shows proposed developments on the estate of Lewis Fenton.* G Redmonds collection

*Murray Road, Edgerton, 1996.* Courtesy of the *Huddersfield Examiner*

development at Edgerton soon afterwards.[38]

It was not long, though, before regret was being expressed for what had been lost. An old boy of Huddersfield College wrote nostalgically in the school magazine of 1878 of a time when 'not a house was to be seen... from the college to Edgerton Bar...' and 'of the lane, now sadly shorn of its homely beauty, endeared to us by the name of Blacker Lane'. He wrote also of 'the road to Edgerton and beyond, now flanked by modern villas' and mourned the loss of 'the glorious horse-chestnut trees with their scented blossoms'. Already, 'the streamlet in the valley below, once so pellucid and attractive' had become 'a filthy watercourse'.

## Gledholt

The poll tax returns of 1379 are invaluable as a list of families and they provide fascinating information about surnames, occupations and status. Occasionally, also, we can use other source material to illustrate the links between some of these families and the way in which their histories are interwoven. There are four Huddersfield families recorded in 1379 that can be dealt with in this way and together they tell us something of the early history of the locality known as Gledholt. Two of the men, John Hirst and William de

Nettleton lived in Quarmby and neither, to judge from the tax they paid, was particularly well off. In Huddersfield, however, lived two men who were comparatively rich, John Gledhowe (or Gledholt), a tailor, and John de Mirfield, a merchant. It is perhaps ironic that the Hirsts and Nettletons survived and even prospered whereas the Gledholts became extinct and the Mirfields declined.

Although all four surnames were already well established in the West Riding in the fourteenth century and the place-name Gledholt is mentioned independently in 1318, the first deed which links the place-name and the surnames is dated 1346. In it Agnes de Bello Monte (Beaumont) made a grant to Joan de Gledholte, William de Mirfeilde and William de Gledholt of 'all her messuages, lands, tenements, meadows, woods, pastures and rights of common lying in a place called Gledholte'.[39] The grant is partly explained by the fact that Joan de Gledholt was formerly the widow of John Beaumont and Agnes was their daughter. The Gledholts had been prominent in Huddersfield since 1296 at least, and they survived until 1379, at which point the name disappears from local records, but a curious aspect of its brief history is that it appears to have been interchangeable in the early 1300s with Gledhill. The variant spelling Gledhowe seems to link it with Allerton Gledhow near Leeds, but there is no evidence of a connection and both these developments are likely to have been scribal errors..

Meanwhile, the Mirfields continued in possession of Gledholt and in 1412 they enfeoffed the property to William de Nettleton. The understanding was that the Nettletons should pay 24s yearly, half at the Feast of St Michael and half at the Nativity. If they fell into arrears Gledholt was to revert to the Mirfields. When this actually happened forty years later the Nettletons were obliged to release the land and the Mirfields acquired a new tenant. The moment is recorded in a document dated 1453 which survives in the Ramsden Deeds and is very similar in its description of the property to the one a century earlier.

> *Know ye that I William de Mirfield have given granted and by these presents have confirmed to William Hirst of Wharneby* [i.e. Quarmby] *draper and Alice his wife, all that messuage aforesaid* [i.e. Gledholt] *with all lands, tenements, woods, meadows, pastures and commons to the same messuage adjoining.*[40]

William Hirst may have been an old man at the time for he died soon after this transaction, but first he made a settlement of Gledholt in favour of two of his sons; Edmund received one third of the property

*Gledholt Chapel from Greenhead Park, 1910.*
G Redmonds collection

and John two thirds. It had been a John Hirst who was taxed at Quarmby in 1379 and this same name was linked with the history of Gledholt for over 200 years. It appears on deeds in 1457, when William's widow released the property to John, and again in 1505 and 1516. In 1524 'John Hirst of the Gledholt' paid 5s tax on his goods valued at £10 and wills bearing exactly the same name and place survive for 1530, 1575, 1602 and 1624. In the hearth tax of 1664 it is something of a surprise to find that the family was represented at Gledholt by an Arthur Hirst.

## Paddock

The meaning of the word 'paddock' has not changed greatly over the centuries and this part of Marsh probably takes its name from a small enclosed piece of ground, although we cannot now identify just where that was. Typical early spellings are 'parock' and 'parrock', hinting at the word's ancient etymological links with 'park', and we have to wait until the late 1700s for the modern spelling to be recorded. The territory's southern boundary was the river and there is known to have been a fulling-mill there from *c.*1500. Nevertheless, the first recorded references to the place-name date from the last thirty years of the sixteenth century, and these make it clear that settlement was scattered between Paddock Foot and Paddock Head. These were almost certainly early encroachments on Marsh common.

*Paddock Head in the 1920s.* Courtesy of the *Huddersfield Examiner*

*The Nab at Paddock Head, 1982.* Courtesy of the *Huddersfield Examiner*

The maps and surveys of Huddersfield manor tell part of the story of Paddock's gradual development through the centuries before the Industrial Revolution, and they identify up to twenty dispersed dwellings, including, for example, John Hodgson's cottage 'at the Nabend' and Lyon Browne's 'good hous at the North side of the Upper end' (1716). There was much more building there in the early 1800s, as the population increased, and by the mid-1800s Paddock found itself at the centre of an acrimonious dispute between Mr Ramsden, the landlord, and many of his tenants. This story has already been told, but less well known is the more modest expansion close to Longroyd Bridge.

## Fenton Square

I referred to the account book kept by Lewis Fenton in 1857 in connection with developments at Blacker Lane but it throws light

*Spring Grove School, built after Spring Grove House was demolished in 1879.*
G Redmonds

also on the Longroyd Bridge area. His property interests included land in Penistone where he had his home, and parts of Huddersfield and Halifax, but wherever he owned land, he liked to put his family name on the map. Consequently, there was Fenton's Court in Halifax, Fenton's Row at Shelf and Fenton's Square at Paddock. The accounts show that he was fully alive to the possibilities of development in all these areas and his comments on the property he owned are fascinating, not least his view of Spring Grove, the old family home built abut 1790.

In 1857 this impressive mansion house had an extensive range of outbuildings, including stables, a cow-house and a coach-house. There were large grounds with ornamental gardens, a small plantation and an impressive carriage drive from the lodge where Benjamin Kenworthy lived. To Lewis Fenton the house was something of a problem and he rented it to Edward Lake Hesp, commenting that he was compelled to take what he could get, for such properties were difficult to let in Huddersfield, largely because the costs of maintenance were so high. He had been obliged, he wrote, to value it as though it was an ordinary tradesman's house.

At the other end of the scale were the cottages he owned in Shelf, several of which were empty, one with the roof fallen in, and generally 'a poor class of buildings'. The farm at Standedge, tenanted by James Murgatroyd, was not much better. The Low Moor Iron Company had sunk a shaft there during the winter in order to extract coal and ironstone and they were paying damages to the tenant for the coal-pit hills and the shaft. However, this was no compensation to Charles Walker who occupied one of the cottages, and against his name in the accounts Mr Fenton wrote: 'The Pit-hill rests against the back of the cottages and make them dampy. He wishes to have it removed'.

His other small pieces of land in Huddersfield form an interesting contrast. He already owned a substantial number of houses at Fenton's Square, having 'fitted up two out-kitchens for eight of the tenants'. He thought it would be an improvement to the large yard if it were railed off and evergreens planted but then, almost as an afterthought, wrote, 'From the smoke of the Neighbourhood, there is some doubt of their being healthy'. However, he had plans for the adjacent piece of steep land which also belonged to him. At that time Jonathon Brook was the tenant and it consisted of rough fields called simply 'Bank'. Nevertheless, Lewis Fenton thought he could 'make available a considerable portion for building purposes, despite the detrimental effect of smoke from Longroyd Bridge' by opening out 'a centre Road from the Bottom of Out-cote Bank and passing along the North side of the Church'. And that is what he did, creating today's Bankfield Road.

On the other side of the town Fenton had property in Birkby. The back part of these premises had been a cropping-shop, but this had been converted into a cottage and kitchen, partly at the expense of the tenant, who had also provided himself with a mistal, a back garden and a greenhouse. These developments contrasted with his Blacker Lane development which he considered to be the most attractive locality in the neighbourhood, one for which the public had 'a decided preference'. In many ways the two can be compared with the major transformations which took place at Moldgreen and Edgerton, one for 'operatives' and the other for successful entrepreneurs.

**An early map of Marsh**

In 1791 Jonathan Teal surveyed the property in Marsh which belonged to John Lister Kaye and drew an attractive plan which shows the settlements at Gledholt and Greenhead.[41] Today's busy

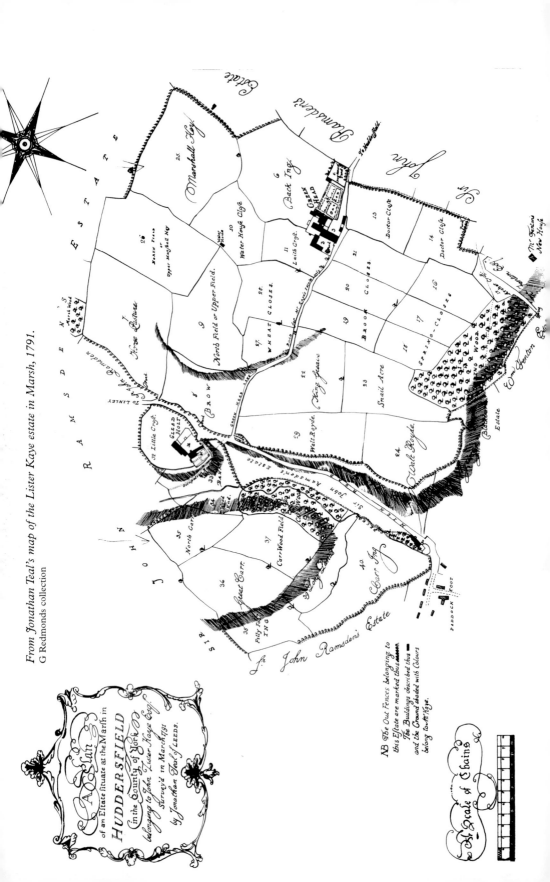

*From Jonathan Teal's map of the Lister Kaye estate in Marsh, 1791.*
G Redmonds collection

*The old footpath from Bow Street to Longroyd Bridge.* G Redmonds

Greenhead Road, which links the two localities, was then a meandering country lane reserved as a 'Private Road for Mr Kaye's estate only', whilst a footpath running south from Greenhead, just outside the fence which defined Mr Kaye's boundary, was on the line of the modern Park Avenue.

Many of the fields shown on the map to the north, Marshall Hey, Horse Pasture and Water House Close, for example, are part of the present Greenhead Park and others which are now suburban streets had such fascinating names as Snail Acre, King Greave and Walt Royde. Marsh Wood has not survived, but Carr Wood and the stream running through it still preserve something of a rural atmosphere. In fact the wood is better known now as T P Woods, a name that has puzzled some Huddersfield people. However, the simple explanation is that Gledholt was home in the 1860s to a local celebrity known as TP to his contemporaries; his full name was Thomas Pearson Crosland and he was the first Conservative MP for the town.

In the south-west corner of the map, marking the boundary with Mr Fenton's property, is the Spring Wood which gave its name to a major local mansion and several more modern streets. The footpath which traversed the wood is mentioned in a Quarter Sessions case of 1728 and it still survives. The victim was Mary Cocker of Dalton who claimed that:

> *...betwixt seven and eight a clock in the afternoon she met Charles Heward on a common called Parrock, who was going towards Millsbridge but turned again and waylayd her at... Spring Wood; when about the middle of the said wood he pull'd her out of the way down into the thick of the wood... and there, after long strugling... us'd his pleasure on her.*

Little of the woodland has survived but the scarcely-known footpath can still be followed all the way to Longroyd Bridge from an obscure entry off Bow Street, crossing the railway en route.

# 3     $\mathcal{F}$ARTOWN

There was considerable expansion in Huddersfield township during the Tudor period, with documentary evidence for up to thirty named settlements, most of them recorded for the first time. A significant number of these were houses built on the waste in Fartown and Deighton, in the eastern half of the township, and many were occupied by members of the Brook family, which ramified in a quite remarkable way. In fact, of ten settlements first recorded in the area in the period 1489-1532, no fewer than seven had a Brook in occupation. Equally interesting, from the point of view of place-names is the fact that eight employed the suffix 'house', i.e. Fieldhouse, Greenhouse, Newhouse, Barkhouse, Blackhouse, Yatehouse, Cloughhouse and Hillhouse. These were scattered through the territories of Cowcliffe, Sheepridge and Fartown which were then areas of waste or common, and their names too were recorded for the first time in the sixteenth century.[42]

There was similar expansion through to the end of the seventeenth century, and the Brooks continued to be more prominent in the district than other families. However, their role was not quite as dominant as it had been earlier and names such as Hirst and Horsfall, which both came from outside the township, were beginning to play their part in the expansion. It was also the case that 'house' ceased to be an important naming element from c.1600 and after that date new settlements tended to be spread over a wider area. A few were still in Sheepridge and Fartown, but there were at least two in Marsh and four in Bradley.

**Bay Hall – two early documents**
Bay Hall was held by John Byron in 1566, the Lord of the Manor, and in a lease to John Brouke that year he described it as the 'manor or haule place called Baihaule'. The lease was for half the premises and it included 'halfe of all the fruit growing in the orchard', as well as the usual arable, meadow and pasture. John was to repair and maintain the house and 'make the same defensible', whilst John Byron undertook to 'delyver sufficient grete tymber for and towards the reparacions'. The terms are fairly typical of leases at that time but less usual was a 'postscript', in a different colour of ink, that required John Brouke 'to fynde an hable man suffycently horssed and harnessed... to attende uppon John Byron' in the event of war.[43]

*Bay Hall, Birkby, 1954.* Courtesy of the *Huddersfield Examiner*

The only earlier reference to the house is in a deed dated 1565, in which the same John Brouke of 'Bayhaull' acted as a witness, but that may imply that the family had been at the hall for some time. As they were tanners, or barkers to use a local word, it is tempting to see a connection with John Brooke of Barkhouse, taxed in 1524, especially as no other reference to that place-name has so far been recorded. The name could have been changed to give the dwelling greater status.

Bay Hall clearly owed its status to the fact that it was the 'manor place' and it is strange, therefore, that the name is so poorly documented. The problem is that the Byron family's manorial records seem not to have survived, so all we know about the earlier history is what the building itself tells us. Nor do we know much about the family itself, for they were absentee landlords, living at Newstead in Nottinghamshire. If the Brooks had a role as the Byrons' stewards in Huddersfield, and that is certainly possible, it might help to explain why they were able to expand so successfully in that part of the township.

Also living at Bay Hall in the 1560s were William and Edmund Brooke, and the latter was taxed £10 in the subsidy of 1570. He was a tanner, like other members of the family, and his will of 2 July 1573 contains numerous items of interest. Even the preamble is a little out of the ordinary:

> *I Edmonde Brooke of Bayhall... sicke in bodie but whole in mynde and enioynge my p(er)fecte memorie do willinglie with a free harte render and give againe into the handes of my lorde my god my sowle whiche he of his fatherlie goodnes gave unto me when he fasyoned this my bodie in my motheres wombe, by this meanes makinge me a levinge Creature...*

After concluding this preliminary section Edmund first made arrangements for his 'mortuary' or gift to the vicar, saying he was determined 'to bestowe the same... in this liffe' with his own hands. He then immediately recited the contents of a detailed deed of conveyance, first in English and then in Latin, which provides us with the names of many of the important fields and meadows close to the centre of the town. He held strips and doles in 'Staynlandbuttes, Townebrowkeynge, Rowghclose, Brodelayes, Litlekirkmore, Bayneclose and Est Mylneroid' – the last-named of these lying 'of bothe side the water of Colne'. He also held a lease of the tithes of hay and corn for Huddersfield, Lindley and Longwood and 'one messuage comonlie caulled Hilhouse', recently purchased from John Byron.

Edmund had a large family and in the will he names at least five sons and two daughters, several of whom were still under age. The estate that he itemised in the deed was conveyed to two men, Thomas Beamonte of Flockton, husband to his daughter Agnes, and Thomas Browke 'of the newehouse', his brother, to be held in trust for a younger son John. The tenants were named as John Armitage, Thomas Sikes, John Turner and Thomas Shaye 'de backside', and there was also an early reference to Thomas Kilner, who operated the fulling mill at what we now call Bradley Mills. The place-name Kilner Bank preserves that association.

Edmund was careful to make provision for his wife Jennett but in the long term Bay Hall itself was to go to his eldest son William, and Hillhouse to Edmund, another younger son. Three other children to receive bequests were Roger, Thomas and Sebell, but they were not yet of age and Jennett was to be responsible for their 'whole governance and custodie'.[44]

## New House Hall
New House Hall is an attractive and historic mansion but it is also something of a symbol. It sits among green fields with its back to the woodlands and we can imagine without too much difficulty the beauty and isolation of the site in the sixteenth century. On the other hand the estates of modern Huddersfield have crept so close to its front that it gives an impression of a house at bay, conscious that it is under threat and not too sure of its future. The outbuildings were the first to suffer, bearing scars from the preliminary skirmishes long before they were demolished.

The house has many stories to tell and much has already been written about its main architectural features and the major families who have lived there in the last four hundred years. In a way though it is the story of its foundation early in the 1500s that is most fascinating, and to understand that we have first to know something of Deighton and Sheepridge in the Middle Ages.

Sheepridge can be dealt with fairly quickly. The earliest references to it always describe it as the 'common of Sheepridge' and make no mention of any inhabitants or settlements. The name itself is suggestive of the part it played in Huddersfield manor and it is surely significant that old farmsteads such as Shepherd's Thorn and Lamb Cote were situated just to the north in Nether Bradley. On the other hand, there has been a settlement at Deighton for at least eight hundred years, although the documents imply that it consisted of a single house even as late as *c*.1520. The only real evidence for that is the family name Deighton, or Dighton as it was more commonly spelt, which is recorded at regular intervals in the township from the late twelfth century to *c*.1350. The Dightons were later the tenants of Ravensknowle in Dalton and also had land in Batley and Woolley, and they continued to be quite prominent in the region until the late 1400s when they sold much of this property. It is possible that their successors at Deighton were the Brooks, for a number of early fifteenth-century documents refer to William by the Brook of Deighton.[45] In fact this is the only other surname associated with the hamlet as late as the 1530s, after which branches of the Hirsts and Steads were also living there.

*New House Hall, Sheepridge, 1988.* Courtesy of the *Huddersfield Examiner*

We do not know exactly when New House was built but if we examine early documents two important points emerge. The first is that when Thomas Brook of Newhouse made his will, in 1554, he bequeathed to his son 'one howse caulled newhowse latelie taken of the west (sic) called Shipridge together with... five acres of land lieinge of the west side the said howse latelie by me builded'.[46] The second point is that pedigrees of the Brooks of Newhouse, admittedly not entirely satisfactory, emphasise a preoccupation in the sixteenth century with the first name Thomas. As a Thomas Brooke of Newhouse was mentioned in a list of Huddersfield clothiers as early as 1533, it is obvious that the house was built before then.

These points seem to throw new light, therefore, on a deed in the Beaumont papers. In 1521 Richard Beaumont of Whitley Hall granted to 'Thomas Brooke of Dyghton, junior, 3 acres of land, with half an acre of land from the common waste called Shepperygge'. The land is then described as 'lying to the west of a gate called Bradley Yatte, to the south of Bradley Wood and to the north of the said

*An old doorway in the barn at New House Hall, 1988. These outbuildings have now been demolished.* Courtesy of the *Huddersfield Examiner*

common', a location that fits exactly with that of New House.[47] The conclusion must be that the house was built on this site soon after 1521 and that the Brookes who lived there were a branch of the Deighton Brooks. This grant by the Beaumonts, followed by others in the next hundred years, seems to have been part of a deliberate policy to enclose parts of the traditional common land. A later lease at New House was in fact granted in consideration of the expenses that Thomas Brook had incurred whilst 'taking in, enclosing, fencing and reducing into husbandry, one piece of barren ground of the wastes and commons of the manor of Huddersfield, called Sheepridge'.[48] It is ironic to reflect that this process of enclosure and development, begun four hundred and fifty years ago, has now reached such dimensions that it threatens to engulf the first house built there.

The original 'new house' was probably a modest-sized, timber-framed building, but this appears to have been entirely swept away in changes effected by Thomas Brook's descendants. One possible change may be hinted at in references after 1590 to 'the nether newhouse' and 'the over newhouse', each occupied by a family called Brook. This might at first seem to imply that there were two houses on the site by then but no other evidence points that way and there are good grounds for believing that New House may just have been drastically remodelled *c.*1590, with the house body incorporated into a stone building. If that was the case Thomas Brooke occupied the 'nether' or lower end and Edward Brooke the 'over' or upper end. The wing destroyed by fire in the nineteenth century was probably a surviving portion of that house.

By 1630 Thomas Brook had acquired the status of 'gentleman' and possessed an estate which included property as far afield as Bingley to the north and Worsbrough to the south. It was probably during those years, towards the end of his life, that he built the surviving west wing where some of the panelling is said to carry his initials. In his will of 1638, in which New House was described as a capital messuage but not a 'hall', the anxiety he felt about his family is clear. He requested his successor Joshua Brook to look after his wife and children 'att his table att Newhouse, with sufficient houseroom and fyreroome, lodgings, meat and drinke suitable to their callings'.[49] The house then may have had the original house body of *c.*1525, flanked by wings of *c.*1590 and *c.*1635.

The surviving hall has numerous interesting features, including a fine staircase and plaster ceilings and, if Colum Giles is correct in saying that it was rebuilt in 1690, the conclusion must be that John Townley was the person responsible.[50] He had previously married

Helen Brook and is known to have resided at New House in the late 1600s. It was there, no doubt, in the new and impressive hall that he carried out many of his magisterial duties. The Quarter Sessions records show that witnesses were interviewed at the house by Mr Townley and their statements prepared by a clerk before being submitted to the courts held at Wakefield and Pontefract. Even then the house seems not to have been called a 'hall', which may mean that it gained that status as late as 1865 when the new owner, John William Ramsden, had the present east wing rebuilt.

### Greenhouse

The present residence called Greenhouse was identified by Edward Law as one of the few buildings on the former Ramsden Estate that was planned by the London architect Edward Blore.[51] Otherwise little has been said about it, even though the history of the site goes back nearly five hundred years. No doubt it takes its name from being a dwelling-house on Fartown Green, but the irony is that it is referred to in local records long before Fartown itself. In 1504 Richard Beaumont of Whitley Hall granted a 24-year lease on 'Greenhowse', at an annual rent of 53s 4d, to a man called James Blagburne, but it is unclear whether he lived there or had a sub-tenant.[52] Certainly the Blackburns at that time were one of the most important families in Huddersfield.

The occupants of the house, for well over a century, were yet another branch of the Brook family, and the first we can identify is the Edmund Brook who was taxed at 'Greynhouse' in 1524, paying 12d on goods valued at 40s. The christian names Edmund and Edward both appear in the records relating to the house between 1524 and 1566, but they could be used interchangeably in the sixteenth century and it is not always clear whether we are reading about two men or just one. It is likely though that the tenant throughout this period was the Edmund Brook who died in 1566 and whose will survives at York. At that time Greenhouse still formed part of the 'moiety' or half of Huddersfield manor that had been granted to the Beaumonts by the de Lacys in *c.*1200 and Edmund Brook's status is clear from the number of manorial documents he was asked to witness. Furthermore, in a lease of 1547, he and James Beaumont were described as 'deputies' of Richard Beaumont, responsible for the management of woods in South Crosland and Meltham.[53] According to the lease the spring woods at Butternab and Colders Clough had been 'set furthe, boundid, lymyted and appoyntid by Edmund Brouke of the Grenhowse'. Of course it would be wrong from this to conclude that wood management was Edmund Brook's only occupation, and both men would be better described as 'yeoman clothiers'. The estate records show that during their time at Greenhouse they farmed the land, growing mostly oats and rye, whilst in 1533 they were named in a list of local clothiers in trouble with the authorities. Other branches of the family, notably John Brook of Bay Hall, were tanners at that time and the likelihood is that most of these men could turn their hands to a variety of tasks.

The Brooks had been prominent in Huddersfield in 1379 and were a prolific family in Fartown right through the sixteenth century, using a relatively small number of first names. Edmund and Roger were both much in favour and this Edmund Brook of Greenhouse was followed by a succession of Roger Brooks, one dying in 1588, another in 1629, and a third living there in 1631, by which time the Beaumonts' share of Huddersfield had passed to the Ramsdens. Eventually, however, the tenancy was acquired by the Horsfalls, another prominent Fartown family, and it was during their occupation that the farm came to be used as a meeting house for Quakers. It may have been used by a congregation during the years of persecution for, as soon as the *Act of Tolerance* was passed in 1689, Edmund Horsfall had the house registered at the Quarter Sessions. The registration was renewed by John Horsfall in 1712.[54]

**Longwood House**
Almost contemporary with New House in its foundation was Longwood House, where John Wesley was a frequent visitor in the 1780s. At that time it was a picturesque old dwelling close to the boundary between Fixby and Huddersfield. In August 1781, having preached at Greetland and Huddersfield, Wesley was a guest there of the Whitacre family and he felt moved to describe the area as 'one of the pleasantest spots in the country'. Sadly, both the house and the pleasant countryside have become victims of Huddersfield's development in the last one hundred years or so. According to Philip Ahier the old house was demolished for the sake of the mineral rights and, more recently, a housing estate has replaced the green fields. Perhaps the only remaining links with the past are the stone-built house close to the old Whitacre home and the short stretch of track leading off Lightridge Road which once ran directly to Longwood House. It now ends rather forlornly at a wooden barrier.

One of the first direct references to Longwood House that I have seen is in a deed of 1608 when John Thornhill of Fixby granted the property to two men. One of these was his younger brother Nicholas

Thornhill and the other was Edward Hanson of Nether Woodhouse. It was described in the deed as 'the messuage called Longwoodhouse, within the township of Huddersfield, in the tenure of Richard Longleye and John Couper'.[55] A tithe account shows that both men were still living there in 1620 but we know that Richard Longleye died soon afterwards for his will was proved at York in 1624.

I have not studied in detail the history of other families who lived at Longwood House in the seventeenth century, but the most prominent were probably the Starkeys and the Armitages. In the next century they were succeeded by the Whitacres who became well-known in Huddersfield as cloth merchants and who were also responsible for the building of Woodhouse Church. It may well be that this close link with Woodhouse, and the family living there, helped to obscure the early history of Longwood House, for there is no doubt that the name was thought by many to be 'Long Woodhouse'. The simpler and more likely explanation is that it was the residence in the sixteenth century of the family with the surname Longwood.

There are several puzzling features in this family's history for there is a quite natural inclination to assume that the surname had its origins in the township of Longwood, in the same parish. Direct proof of a link is lacking but one strong piece of circumstantial evidence is in a grant of land at Nettleton Hill in Longwood, witnessed by Edmond Longwod in 1563.[56] Indeed, the surname Longwood is found locally for just short of one hundred years, i.e. *c.*1485-1570, so it either stabilised very late or had an origin outside the area. The only support for the second of these alternatives is that Longwood was an occasional variant of the Lancashire surname Longworth but this seems an unlikely source.

The first recorded member of the family was John Longwodd, fined at Rastrick court in 1485, but, in 1523, Richard Beaumont of Whitley Hall granted to Robert Longwood several 'parcels of land lying in Huddersfield containing about nine acres... between the closes of John Briom (Biron?) on the west and the common called Sheperige on the east and north, and a lane on the south'. He was to pay 2s 8d rent and this probably marks the date when the first Longwood House was built. In 1547, for example, a grant between the sons of the above Robert Longwood referred to the property as 'a messuage with land, in Huddersfield, formerly waste'. Other deeds of 1554 confirm the land-holding as being in the region of nine or ten acres and the rent as 2s 8d. Finally, in 1565, a series of five deeds records the conveyance of Longwood House from Robert Longwood to John Thornhill of Fixby, after which the family appear to have left the neighbourhood.[57]

Very little else is known about them. John Longwood was the constable for Rastrick on a number of occasions, starting in 1524, as was Edmond Longwood as late as 1564, and these dates coincide with the period during which the family owned Longwood House. During the same period their names also appear in local wills and inventories, including that of John Thornhill of Fixby in 1567. There are, of course, other references to the family in that period and these confirm that the Longwoods enjoyed considerable status and had property interests in other places besides Huddersfield. Unfortunately, they shed no real light on how the surname originated. The family may have moved to Knottingley in the late 1560s since the surname is found there long after the connection with Longwood House was broken.

## Birkby

Birkby, which is not a unique place-name in Yorkshire, has several times been offered as evidence of Scandinavian settlement in Huddersfield parish. The two other Yorkshire places with this name, both recorded in the Domesday Book as *Bretebi*, mean the farmstead of the Britons: because the suffix 'by' is a Norse word it has been said

*St John's Church, Birkby, c.1900. The corn field is now part of the industrial estate.*
Clifford Stephenson

*An old house on Birkby Hall Road, now demolished, possibly the original Birkby Hall.* Clifford
Stephenson

that the Britons in these cases must have entered Yorkshire in the tenth century, along with Norwegians moving from the north-west. The meaning of Huddersfield's Birkby must remain in doubt, for there is no evidence that the place-name has an equally long history. Indeed, no record of it has been found until the sixteenth century, when a spelling such as Byrkebye (1561) could equally well be interpreted as 'birch – farmstead'. To complicate matters even further two of the earliest references appear to spell the place-name 'Kirkby.'

The lack of early evidence at least helps to establish that Birkby was initially a relatively unimportant settlement site, surrounded by common or waste. Even as late as the seventeenth century the place-name was still considered to apply to one house only and, even after the beginning of the Industrial Revolution, it consisted of a mere handful of scattered dwellings. Later, it was deemed to have boundaries which included farmsteads such as Storth, and then intensive building during the Industrial Revolution finally helped it to become one of Huddersfield's few genuine suburbs.

We know of no more than half a dozen families who played any part in the early history of the hamlet and not surprisingly this total included the Brooks and the Hirsts, the best-known Huddersfield names of the period. George Brook of Birkby is mentioned in the parish registers in the 1560s and he died in 1586. We know very little about him except that when Huddersfield's commons were being enclosed he was responsible for taking in one acre at the 'netherend of stonielie'. The widow of Edward Brook took in a further acre 'lying on the sunside' of the same common.[58] The area known as Stony Lee is clearly shown on the estate map of 1716 and is remembered now in the name Lee Head. A house of this name was the home of John Brook in 1589.

The Hirsts settled in Birkby much later that the Brooks. Arthur Hirst seems to have been the first to arrive, possibly from Gledholt where a Hirst family also favoured Arthur as a first name. In 1657 there was trouble between these two families but the details are not clear. Thomas Brook was attacked and wounded by Richard Hirst of Clough House, so severely according to one source that he was 'in danger of death'; Arthur Hirst's view, however, was that it was only 'a slight wound'.[59]

A rare surname which found its way into Birkby was Hesslegreave, possibly from Saddleworth where the family lived between *c.* 1300 and 1559 and where the Ramsdens had property for a time. John Hesylgreave died in 1561, but a lease of 1578 in the Ramsden papers granted a house 'at Burkeby' to Isabel his widow and, on her death,

*Fletchers' nursery, Birkby Hall Road, c.1910.* Courtesy of the *Huddersfield Examiner*

to John their son. Exactly where they lived is not certain, but a marriage settlement of 1622 names a third John Hesslegreave, the tenant of a house called 'Thurdlebrough' which it is not possible now to locate or even to explain.[60] Mentioned in the same deed was another house 'called Botheroides', which doubtless took its name from John Botherode of Birkby who held the lease in 1578. Neither of these place-names survived, but in 1622 'Botheroides' was tenanted by Edmond Brook and Elizabeth Botheroid, another widow. Indeed, widows or unmarried women seem to have held most of the property in Birkby in 1622: Joan Midwood was the tenant of 'all that messuage...called Birkbye' and also of another house known as 'Clayes' (probably the home originally of Robert Clay, who died in 1555), whilst Elizabeth Brook held 'Netherhouse' and the corn mill attached to it.

The properties in Birkby and Bay Hall appear to have belonged to the Byrons and the Beaumonts in the sixteenth century, and both families had manorial rights. However, we are still unclear about the exact way in which the estate was shared, although the non-resident Byrons are said to have used Bay Hall as their manor house and there was a manorial corn mill near by. Later, of course, the Ramsdens came into possession of most of Huddersfield, purchasing the manor from the Byrons in 1599 and the Beaumonts' substantial holding almost thirty years later. As most of Huddersfield's development followed on these moves, it is fascinating to speculate what might have become of Bay Hall and Birkby if they had remained in divided ownership.

### Netheroyd Hill

Netheroyd Hill is a difficult place-name to deal with. The modern spelling suggests a meaning such as 'lower-clearing hill', but this is very misleading. In fact the 'nether' part of the word is a fairly recent development and throughout the period c.1550-c.1700 Nathroyd or Naithroyd were the usual forms. However, even the earlier spellings which I have just quoted may be distortions of the original place-name. In a surviving fragment of court roll for Huddersfield, dated 1532, a tenant called John Broke was said to have encroached a piece of land from the waste at Nase Rode,[61] and the circumstances suggest that this was the area later known as Nathroyd or Netheroyd Hill.

If this identification is correct, and an occasional later spelling such as Nazroyd suggests that it is, then the meaning poses no problems. The Old English words 'naess' and 'nasu' (modern English nose) were used quite frequently in the Middle Ages for prominent headlands and would have been very appropriate in this case. Perhaps most difficult to accept is the linguistic development from 'Nase' to 'Nathe', but there are other examples of this change, and the similarities between the two sounds are obvious, particularly if we consider the problems that both French and Germans experience with our 'th'.

The Netheroyd Hill area formed part of the vast extent of common or waste to the north of Huddersfield and it was certainly not a habitative place-name to begin with. The first families actually to settle there were the Brooks and the Batleys, who both enclosed land from the common in the 1500s and lived at a hamlet known as Stone Delves. This place-name is evidence in itself that quarrying must have been carried on there for well over four hundred years and the impact that had on the landscape is apparent, even though most of the

*Netheroyd Hill in the early 1900s.* Clifford Stephenson

quarry sites are now overgrown. Confirmation of the importance of 'stone-getting' in the area can be found in the Fartown surveyors accounts; these include 'Raleing Stone Delf' (1759) and 'filling a delf on Netheroyd Hill' (1789).[62]

Another interesting reference to Netheroyd Hill occurs in the West Riding Sessions Rolls for 1671, when Anthony Allison, a poor man with a large family, petitioned the court saying that he had 'sustained diverse losses and was likely to bee put out of his house'. In consequence, he had sought and obtained permission of the Lord of the Manor 'to build a cottage upon the Comon, neare Stone delves, Called Naithroyd Hill'. The request was granted by the court, and we can imagine that his home was close to the spot later known as Allison Dyke.

In the eighteenth century more houses and cottages were built in this area. In 1706 Joshua Keighley signed a certificate 'allowing

widow Armitage 'to build a cottage near Nathroyde'[63] and a rental for
1716 names Widow Sikes as the tenant of 'Cottages called follyhall at
Stonedelphs'.[64] In 1771 Thomas Brook, Joseph Cliffe and John
Howroyd all had new cottages there[65] and in 1780 Sir William
Ramsden leased land on Netheroyd Hill to the Whitacres on which
they had built a drying house.[66] Another family to settle in the area in
the eighteenth century were the Netherwoods, and it seems likely that
it was their surname, so close in pronunciation to Netheroyd in
colloquial speech, which determined the modern form of Netheroyd
Hill. The Census Returns for 1861 show clearly how the two names
influenced each other, i.e. George and Henry Neatheroyd of
Neatheroyd Hill.

Stone Delves now seems to have died out as a specific place-name
and Netheroyd Hill is usually thought of as the 'village' name but the
street names Allison Drive and Netherwood Close serve to remind us
of two of the families who played a role in the history of this small
community.

## Moldwarp Hall

Moldwarp is an old north country word for the common mole,
meaning something like 'earth-thrower', but it is now seldom heard.
Our ancestors had an ambivalent attitude towards the animal, valuing
it for its fur which was used for making hats, but seeing it also as a
pest which threw up unwanted mounds of earth wherever it travelled.
The word has a long pedigree in Yorkshire and I have found
references in old records to 'one mold warppe hatt' (1570) and to 'the
mouldwarpe catcher' (1617), and there was 'land called
Molewerphill' near Ackton in 1478.

The place-name is first recorded in Huddersfield in 1771, when a
tenant named Henry Hey paid £1 16s 0d for 'a house called
Mouldwarp Hall and a close near Longwood House'.[67] During the
tenancy of Elizabeth Hey, early in the 1800s, the name became first
of all Molewarp Hill and then Mole Hill, but it has now reverted to
the original name. It took Mockbeggar Hall in Mirfield rather longer
to be shortened to Mock Hall, but doubtless the motivation in each
case was the same – a desire to be rid of a name that might cause
amusement. It may be though that the name was initially meant to be
amusing, for it can be compared with a number of other local names.

The reason I say this is that we can see a pattern locally to the use
of the word 'hall' in place-names. In the Middle Ages it was used only
of the great houses of the gentry and nobility but then, in the Tudor
period, it became quite common for a status conscious yeoman or

*Moldwarp Hall, a rural setting just off the main Bradford Road.* Tony Burke

clothier to call his house a 'hall', possibly in the hope that the name would suggest to others that he was a member of the gentry. The third group of 'hall' names are those which were coined from the late 1700s, and typical Yorkshire examples include Mushroom Hall, Tewit Hall and Squirrel Hall. More locally we have Bracken Hall, Lamb Hall, and Laverock (i.e. lark) Hall, names given to modest dwellings which were built on the wastes and commons of the manor, sometimes without permission. The fact that so many of the names were drawn from the fauna and flora of the commons suggests that the tenant-builders were allowing themselves a quiet smile at the social climbing of their better-off neighbours.

*The* Ash Brow, *Bradford Road. The valley to the east was once called Cuckold Clough.* Tony Burke

## Ash Brow

There are numerous localities in and around Huddersfield with names such as Oak(es) or Ash(es) and, from one point of view, that hardly seems surprising. After all, the oak and the ash have for centuries been two of the major hardwood trees native to the district. Indeed, some of the trees that we are now equally familiar with, particularly the sycamore and the horse chestnut, have been introduced into this area within the period of written history, and their influence on place-names has been negligible.

However, the very fact that the oak and the ash were so prolific in the past may seem to be an argument against their validity as place-names, and it seems reasonable to look for an explanation of why they were so commonly used. One point worth considering is that in the earlier phases of clearance and settlement, where an individual tree or a small group of trees had been left standing, these readily served as boundary markers, or as shelter for an isolated dwelling. In the latter case it is easy to understand how the house itself would soon come to be known as 'the oaks' or 'the ashes'.

Several of the very earliest minor settlements in the Huddersfield area had names of this type, suggesting that they were established in the great woodland clearance of the thirteenth and fourteenth centuries. This is true of Oakes in Rastrick, Oakes in Almondbury and Oakes in Lindley, all of which were also used as by-names or surnames in the 1300s. Oakes in Lindley lay close to the highway leading to Milnsbridge and was being called Highgate Oakes as early as 1600. This now survives as the name of a public house.

Evidence of the uses to which solitary trees were put by our ancestors can often be found in old documents. A twelfth century description of the boundaries of the lands held by Fountains Abbey in Bradley, for example, refers to 'the old oak on the hillock marked with a cross', whilst in a dispute over riverside pastures at Rastrick, in 1625, much of the testimony was concerned with a single 'Ashe tree... felled and cut down within the memory of man'.[68]

*A map of the Calder at Rastrick, 1625, showing the ash tree that was at the heart of the boundary dispute.* G Redmonds collection

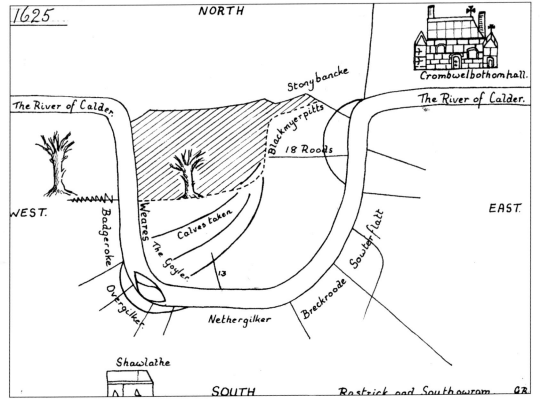

Grange Ash was the site of an inn on the highway near Denby, now replaced by the *Kaye Arms*, and it may go back well before 1577-79 when it is first recorded on Saxton's map of Yorkshire. It is actually on the former Grange Moor where Byland Abbey had land and could originally have been a boundary marker, named after a solitary ash that had survived early clearance. That is pure speculation but, whether it is true or not, the presence of an ash on the waste invites us to consider carefully just what the word 'moor' meant to our ancestors.

There is one example locally of a single tree giving rise to a place-name which is reasonably well documented. On Sheepridge common there was formerly a solitary dwelling called Cuckold Clough which took its name from a deep-cut valley that is still a noticeable feature of the landscape. The name now appears to be extinct and the inference is that it has been replaced by Ash Brow, which seems to have had its origin soon after 1543. A tenant called James Mellor took a lease that year on 'the messuage called Cokewold Clough' and he and his descendants held the property for a considerable time.[69] By 1565 they had expanded the holding, for one of the title deeds to the property refers to 'land latlye enclosed of the waste'.[70]

In 1633, after the Mellors had departed, this small estate was described as 'lying upon a place called Sheepridge, of which ten acres doth abut upon Meller Ashe', that is Mellor's ash tree.[71] By 1789, when the common was finally being enclosed, the Act of Parliament refers to 'the common called Ashbrow, across a valley called Cuckolds Clough'. Today the name Ash Brow refers both to the district and to a public house which stands beside the nineteenth century turnpike road from Bradford, no doubt close to where there was once an ash tree marking the limit of James Mellor's newly-won land.

# *C*OMMUNICATIONS

The traveller who stands today in the centre of Huddersfield has a very clear idea of which roads he would take to the nearest big towns and in every case the route would be substantially different from the one followed by our ancestors in the seventeenth and eighteenth centuries. Even those local people who are aware of the changes that have taken place and know about the so-called 'old' highways, are probably thinking mainly of developments during the Turnpike era.

The Old Halifax Road through Grimescar, for example, is no older than 1777, and we know from the Quarter Sessions records that local clothiers had previously had a much more difficult journey. In 1652 the Huddersfield overseer of the highways had neglected to repair that earlier road and attention was drawn to his omission in an

*The guide stoop on Lindley Moor, 1755. The surveyor was Abraham Mallinson and pointed fingers direct the traveller to Brighouse, Milnsbridge, Marsden and Halifax.*
Tony Burke

*Cowcliffe Hill, a steep climb on the former road to Halifax.* Tony Burke

indictment which called it the 'high and publike way leading
betweene Hothersfeild and the market Towne of Hallifax, in a
certaine place called Cawkliffe'.[72] The road led then across open
country, for Cowcliffe Common was still heath or moorland, and the
traveller's attention was drawn to the route by Cowcliffe Cross, the
base of which survives near the top of the hill in a characteristic
situation. The oldest route that we know of over Cowcliffe, was called
in the court rolls 'the upper waye leadinge betweene Huddersfield
and Eland' and it actually ran 'alonge by Fekisbie hall' in 1639,
making for the farm called 'over coate'.[73]

It is difficult now to accept that in those days the traveller setting
out for Leeds, Bradford or Halifax would initially have taken the
same route across the common at the bottom of town, 'the Nether
Green'. This was roughly on the line of the present Leeds road but

then turned abruptly left at Hillhouse Lane, now closed to through traffic. At Hillhouse the ways diverged and those people aiming for Bradford or Leeds would have continued forwards to Fartown Green and so up Woodhouse Hill to Sheepridge Cross. No trace of this monument survives but it is referred to in old documents. The road over Sheepridge Common was described in the Quarter Sessions indictment books in 1712 as 'the highway leading between Huthersfeild and Bradley' and it was said to be in such a bad state in the part called 'Dighton Lane' that travellers could not pass that way with their horses and carts without great danger. However, as these same words were used whenever repairs were necessary it would be unwise to take them too literally.

It is made clear later in this section, in the accounts of Somerset Bridge and Longroyd Bridge, how important river crossings formerly were, and the history of the routes to the south of the town demonstrates how even modest affluents of the Colne affected communications. There was no bridge at Waterloo until 1819, so the traveller going to Wakefield followed the present route only as far as the cross at Moldgreen and then had to turn up the hill to the south-east. This route was defined in Quarter Sessions records in 1723, as going up Almondbury Bank, along Almondbury Town Street and then down Fenay Lane.[74] Almost one hundred years were to pass

*The old toll house on Bradley Lane.* Courtesy of Kirklees Cultural Services

before this long pull over the hills could be avoided.

On the River Holme it was Lockwood Bridge that was frequently mentioned in the rolls, notably in 1653 when 'by Vyolence of the water [it] was utterly cast downe and overthrowne'.[75] In 1706, when it had again been 'taken down by...great floods' it was said to carry 'a great Road, very usefull for the Country'.[76] Just as the turnpike to Woodhead in Cheshire was being built, in 1768, it was described as lying 'in the highway leading from the town of Huddersfield to... Holmfirth'. The river was named as 'a rivulet called Holmfirth water, or Honley water or Lockwood water'.[77]

Armitage Bridge marks another crossing of the River Holme and is probably the bridge referred to in the foundation deed of the house known as the 'Armitage', dating to the period 1236-58.[78] There are other references to it through the sixteenth and seventeenth centuries, but it is the petition for a new stone bridge in 1756 that alerts us to its former importance. It was described then as lying in two great roads; the first of these linked Huddersfield with Woodhead in Cheshire, via Holmfirth and Honley, and the second carried traffic from Lancashire to Wakefield. This highway was described as passing through Marsden and 'several other towns' en route to Almondbury and Wakefield, and a glance at the map makes it clear that Ladyhouse Lane was part of the road.[79] Just three years later the Act for the Wakefield and Austerlands Turnpike placed Huddersfield firmly on that route.

### Huddersfield and Woodhead Turnpike

One of the most important factors in the growth of the northern towns was the development of improved communications. The old highways, particularly those across the Pennines, were often inadequate for the increasing volume of wheeled traffic and it was becoming clear by the early 1700s that something had to be done. The first step was for interested parties, composed of local gentry, manufacturers and merchants, to promote Acts of Parliament giving them the power to create new Turnpike Roads. Manchester men were quick off the mark and, between 1732 and 1735, they turnpiked the Woodhead highway as far as Saltersbrook and the Standedge route as far as Austerlands, bringing both roads up to the county boundary.

The West Riding response was slow and it was not until 1759 that the road between Wakefield and Austerlands was built, improving Huddersfield's links with Manchester. The road to Woodhead had to wait even longer and it was 1768 before an Act was passed granting the parties concerned the necessary powers. Sadly most of the important documents relating to this road appear to have been lost

*Armitage Bridge, 1995, on an early route to Lancashire.*
Courtesy of the *Huddersfield Examiner*

*Folly Hall at the bottom of Chapel Hill. It was built in 1775 for Marmaduke Hebden, one of the major promoters of the turnpike road to Woodhead in Cheshire. Demolished 1906.* Courtesy of the *Huddersfield Examiner*

but one small item has survived and it tells us a great deal. It is headed 'The present state of the Turnpike road from Huddersfield to Woodhead, 24 September 1774' and it tells us that the improvements made possible by the Act of 1768 had been carried out quickly. Tolls had already been collected from 17 February 1769 and the average yearly income after that was about £130. This was almost entirely from tolls collected at Lockwood Bar, although a small sum was also collected from Woodhead Bar in August 1774.

Many of the sixteen names on the list of subscribers belonged to families settled in the Holme Valley, including Haighs, Walkers, Armitages, the Greens of Greenhouse and the Wilsons of Holmfirth. The only Huddersfield man was Marmaduke Hebden and the only woman was Miss Firth of Clough House. Two men came from much further away – Thomas Bradley from Leeds and William Creswick from Macclesfield, and their names emphasise the value of the link to manufacturers over a much wider area. The two prominent landowners involved were the Rt Hon Lord Dartmouth and Sir John Ramsden, Bt. Important financial contributions came from John Haigh and Joseph Armitage of Honley, both giving £200, and the smallest sum was £20 from Joseph Robinson of Holme. Green and Wilson had both advanced significant sums but these had not yet found their way into the accounts. It was cautiously stated that 'in case they amount to their full subscriptions these will be to add', i.e. £214 16s. The largest investment was £224 by Marmaduke Hebden, who further showed his faith in the town by building a three-storey warehouse at the foot of what we now call Chapel Hill. The line of the highway passed mostly through green fields and the meeting house that gave Chapel Hill its name had not yet been built, so Mr Hebden's contemporaries called the warehouse Folly Hall and that no doubt reflects their scepticism. A final point of interest is Sir John Ramsden's sum of £105 'for land taken into the road'.[80]

The speed with which the new road had been brought into service does not suggest that vast improvements had taken place. Doubtless the road surface was better but it is unlikely that the line of the route itself had changed very much. W B Crump described the West Riding turnpikes of this period as 'timid in conception and unsuitable for wheeled traffic'. In fact, it was not until 1809 that the route from Lockwood to Honley was built along the valley bottom, and the stretch of road which crosses Holme Moss remains a formidable obstacle even today. It probably retains much of the character of an early turnpike because of the more direct route opened up from Holmfirth to Saltersbrook at the time of the 1830 Enclosure award.

*Cooper Bridge, Bradley, 1930.* Courtesy of Kirklees Cultural Services

## Huddersfield Bridges

The River Calder forms the boundary of Huddersfield parish to the north and the River Colne separates it from Almondbury parish in the south, a location which emphasises how important bridges are likely to have been in the town's development. There are documentary references to Colne Bridge and Cooper Bridge, both with attachments in Bradley, in the twelfth-century records of Fountains Abbey, and their later status as 'County' bridges no doubt owes much to that early connection. The fact that Cooper Bridge was originally 'Cowforth' Bridge suggests that it had replaced an even older 'forth' or ford across the Calder at that point. Two other bridges, much closer to the town centre, i.e. Somerset Bridge and Longroyd Bridge, are not mentioned until much later and were of a lower status. The challenges to that status, made by Huddersfield inhabitants in the seventeenth and eighteenth centuries, reflect the growing importance of the town, particularly after the granting of the market charter.

### Somerset Bridge

This bridge has had several names in the course of its history, starting with 'Huddersfeld Bridg' in 1537. Much later it was called Long Bridge, a name which gave way to Somerset Bridge after its rebuilding in 1874, when Lady Guendolen Ramsden performed the opening ceremony. She was the third and youngest daughter of the Duke of Somerset.

Although a good deal has already been written about this bridge,[81] not much has been said about the disputes over its status, so the discovery of new material that throws some light on the topic is of particular interest. The document in question is a letter in the Spencer/Stanhope papers in Bradford archives, and it was written by Walter Stanhope and John Harrison in June 1621, addressed to 'all the several Constables within the parish of Giesley'. They were being requested to 'collect and gather... such voluntarie benevolence and contribution, as all well affected persons shall thinke good to bestowe towards the edifying and building againe of Huddersfield Bridge', which had been 'taken awaye by the violence of a greate flood'.

*Huddersfield 'Long' Bridge, shortly before its demolition in 1872. The temporary wooden bridge is clearly visible.* Courtesy of Kirklees Cultural Services

The first point of interest here is that Guiseley was being asked to pay something towards the rebuilding, for it was a parish in Skyrack Wapentake, many miles to the north of Huddersfield. In fact, it was requested that the letter should be forwarded to the various townships in the parish, and a list on the reverse side of the document records a number of cash contributions from Guiseley, Esholt, Yeadon and Horsforth. The sum contributed was five shillings, which may not sound very much, but the principle involved is very important indeed: Huddersfield Bridge was a Wapentake Bridge, that is to say it was traditionally repaired at the expense of the Wapentake of Agbrigg and Morley. The fact that money was now being solicited outside the Wapentake suggests that certain influential people must have been seeking to place it on a par with 'County' Bridges such as Colne Bridge and Cooper Bridge.

The suspicion must be that the Ramsdens of Longley Hall were at least partly responsible, for the instructions in the letter say that the money should 'be sent to William Ramsden, Esquier who is to see the same bestowed'. If such efforts were repeatedly being made by the local gentry, it may explain certain puzzling statements made at the Quarter Sessions in 1648, the year when John Ramsden contracted with workmen to carry out repairs to the bridge. They pleaded that the work had already been completed but that no money to pay them had been forthcoming, despite an order of the court. As a result it was then further ordered that £30 should be raised from the whole West Riding and 'paid to the hands of those that disbursed the moneys'. However, the officers of the court also stressed that Huddersfield Bridge was only a Wapentake Bridge and the court's decision should be seen 'as a benevolence onely'. It must not, they said, be used 'to bynd the said Ryding to repaire the said bridge hereafter'.[82] The two pieces of evidence seem to point towards an on-going disagreement over the importance of Huddersfield Bridge to the West Riding.

The 1621 document supported the request for money from Guiseley parish with a claim that the bridge was part of 'the usuall waye for th'inhabitants of Doncaster, Bawtrie, Tickhill and those partes, for their trading into Lancashire and Cheshire'. Ogilby's map of 1675 shows it as the crossing of the Colne in the major highway between London and Richmond in the north. The route into Lancashire certainly maintained its importance for it was turnpiked in 1759 between Wakefield and Austerlands. No doubt the local population felt somewhat aggrieved at being held responsible for a bridge which was being used by so much through traffic and the letter

of 1621 emphasises that aspect of the matter, pointing out that
Huddersfield's inhabitants were responsible for no fewer that 'neine
other Bridges'.

There is one final reference in the Spencer/Stanhope document
which may throw new light on the bridge itself. We already know that
it was made of wood at that time and, according to the writers of the
letter, it was 'fiftie five yeards in length', apparently very much longer
than the modern bridge. It has often been said that in earlier
centuries the valley suffered regularly from floods, and much of the
land on both sides of the river would have been extremely marshy.
Clearly those areas would pose a formidable obstacle to travellers,
and a bridge that was fifty-five yards long seems to emphasise that
point. No doubt that measurement included causeways at each end
of the bridge which would have had sluices for the passage of flood
waters. There are surviving Yorkshire bridges from that period which
offer us a much clearer idea of what it might have looked like.

### Longroyd Bridge

Little has been written about the early history of Longroyd Bridge,
although it was an important crossing of the River Colne on the
major route between Huddersfield and Manchester. Crump
described it as a Wapentake bridge, to be maintained, therefore, at the
expense of Agbrigg and Morley Wapentake, but it did not originally
have that status and so is not automatically documented in the first
Quarter Sessions Records. Nevertheless, it is mentioned by name in
a variety of early sixteenth century deeds, for example, as
'longroidebrigg' (1501)[83] and 'longroydbrygge' (1519).[84]

In 1597, when the bridge was stated to be in great decay, a
dispute arose as to who was responsible for its maintenance and the
matter was brought to the attention of the Justices of the Peace. The
evidence given by witnesses is enlightening about its status,
particularly the description of its position 'betwene the Townships
of Huddersfeild and Quarmebie'.[85] This serves to remind us that a
considerable area of land in North Crosland, on the south side of
the river, then formed part of Quarmby township although it lay in
the parish of Almondbury. It is not surprising, perhaps, that
responsibility for the upkeep of the bridge was in dispute, but the
total expense was only £3 8s 2d and Huddersfield's refusal to pay
half of that is an indication of how strongly they felt about the issue.
Finally, the two townships were ordered to settle their differences
by having Mr Robert Kaye of Woodsome exercise his discretion in
the matter.

*Colne Bridge, Bradley. Its structure is very similar to the bridge demolished in Huddersfield in 1872.* G. Redmonds

There are other occasional references to the bridge in the Quarter Sessions as, for example, in 1700 when it was again described as ruinous, and in 1741 when it was said to be on the highway to Rochdale. However, the most illuminating reference is in 1721, when a large number of local people made out a case for the bridge to be given Wapentake status, hoping thereby to diminish the burden on ratepayers from Huddersfield and Quarmby. Their petition is worth quoting in detail for the light it throws on Huddersfield's growth, not just its increasing importance as a market town, but its trade links with other districts and the nature of the traffic then using the pre-turnpike highway.

*...at a place called Longroyd Bridge, about half a mile above Huddersfield in the High road from Manchester, Macclesfield, Stockport, Liverpool, Chester, Northwich, Nantwich and diverse other places in Wales, Lancashire, Cheshire and Stafford, to Leeds, York, Wakefield and other places in the County of York, lyeth an Antient Wood bridge, which by reason of the frequent Passage of Packhorses and other carriages from all parts of the Country for many Miles above the said Bridge and more perticularley since that Huddersfield became a Markett Towne, is now (though all possible care and endeavours from time to time hath been used by your Petitioners to uphold and maintaine the same) in so bad and decayed a Condition that there is an absolute necessity to rebuild the same (the said River at that place being upon every small raine unfordable) which your Petitioners are not able to do, the same upon a moderate Computation by able and skilfull workmen being as appears by the perticulers annext vallued at one hundred and fifty three pounds fifteen shillings and fourpence halfpeny.*[86]

It is certainly interesting to discover that the bridge was still made of wood in 1721, since so many others locally were of stone by that time, and at first it seems surprising that such an important bridge, busy with traffic from over the Pennines, had for so long remained a parish responsibility. Although some of the through traffic may once have avoided Huddersfield altogether, it would not be very long before the growing importance of the route would be recognised with the building of the Wakefield to Austerlands Turnpike.

# 𝓑RADLEY

**B**radley means simply a broad clearing in the woodland and originally it was the name of a township to the north-east of Huddersfield, in the angle of land where the Colne flows into the Calder. In the past it was often called Nether Bradley, in contrast to Over Bradley in Stainland, possibly because the Savile family had interests in both places. Although it lies on the natural route into Huddersfield from Bradford and Leeds in the north, there was no direct road through the Colne Valley in the Middle Ages, and the traditional highway into Huddersfield was over the hills, through Deighton and Woodhouse. Other major routes took travellers either south over the Colne and through Upper Heaton, or passed along Bradley Lane en route to Fixby, Elland and beyond. There is no nucleated 'village' of Bradley and, perhaps because of that, little has been written about it, even though some of the best 'bottom' land in the Huddersfield area lies within its boundaries.

We are now accustomed to thinking of Bradley as a 'hamlet' or part of Huddersfield,[87] but there is no doubt that the two places were quite distinct and separate at the time of the Domesday survey in 1086, and this almost certainly implies that they were independent communities throughout the several hundred years of their history as Anglian settlements. It is, therefore, a matter of some interest to determine, as nearly as possible, just when Bradley was absorbed into Huddersfield and to suggest reasons why it should have lost its independence.

There are many charters relating to the territory in the immediate post-Conquest period. For example, we know that in 1166 it formed part of a knight's fee which Ralph, son of Nicholas de Cridling held from Henry de Lacy II, and that it was recorded as a 'vill' or township in 1219.[88] On the other hand, in the subsidy roll of 1524 Huddersfield cum Bradley was treated as a single township, with Arthur Pilkington, the Lord of Bradley, taxed on lands valued at £40.[89] Clearly, the amalgamation must have taken place between those two dates and there are good reasons for thinking that it may have happened in the earlier part of the thirteenth century.

For example, Bradley was not included as an independent township in either the subsidy roll of 1297 or the poll tax of 1379 and, in the latter of these rolls, the return for Huddersfield included the name of John de Grenewode, who paid 12d as the 'Farmer of the

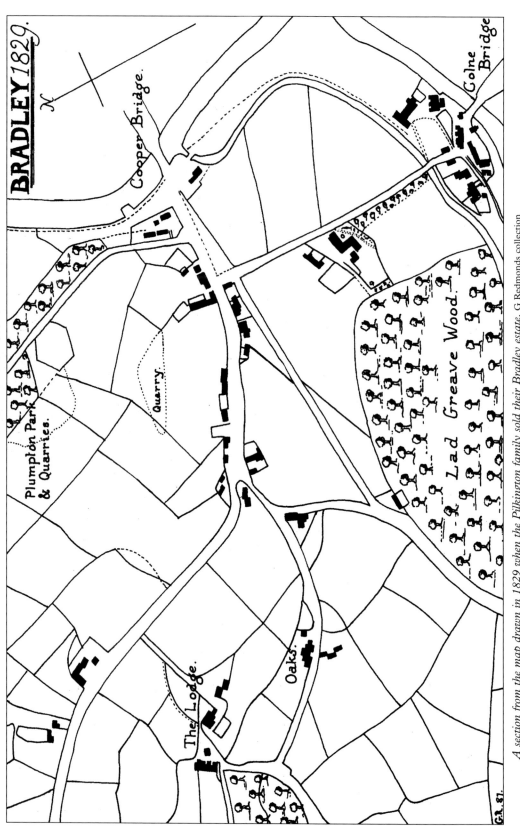

*A section from the map drawn in 1829 when the Pilkington family sold their Bradley estate. G Redmonds collection*

*The* White Cross Inn, *Bradley, in the early 1900s.* Clifford Stephenson

Grange'. This must surely have referred to Bradley Grange, an outpost of Fountains Abbey, and it is this connection which seems likely to account for the loss of township status.

We know that in the second half of the twelfth century much of the territory in Bradley was granted to Fountains Abbey by Ralph, son of Nicholas, the landowner mentioned earlier. In fact, there has been speculation that he was actually a descendant of the man named Chetel who had held Bradley of the de Lacys in 1086. Whether or not that is so it was the sequence of grants by this family and their tenants that allowed the monks to build up a large estate in and around Bradley, one which was estimated later to be over 4,000 acres, and which they proceeded to develop immediately. The abbey was certainly responsible for the erection of bridges over the Calder and the Colne by 1185 and, not long afterwards, a corn-mill was built on the latter river, the mill-stones being quarried in the Crosland area. Even earlier, in 1177, the monks were also taking advantage of a grant which allowed them exclusive rights to forges in Bradley Wood and 'all the ironstone they could find'. It may even have been the ironstone which had first attracted their interest.[90]

Although we do not know exactly when Bradley Grange was set up as the abbey's local headquarters, a confirmation grant establishes that it was already there in the reign of Richard I, so it may well have been built at the time of the first major land grants, a generation earlier. There seems no reason to doubt that the grange then enjoyed considerable prosperity and success, despite disputes with Nostell Priory over tithes, and periodic squabbles with the officials and tenants of Wakefield manor. In fact, the township's loss of status seems likely to have occurred in that period. Twelfth century charters for Bradley contain the names of numerous tenants and their substantial holdings, but these cannot be traced in later sources and the inference is that much of the area must have been depopulated as the abbey organised its lands in that part of Huddersfield into a grange estate.[91]

However, we learn from surviving documents that as early as 1310 the bridge over the Calder, which started out as the 'cow ford' but is now known as Cooper Bridge, was in a dangerous state of disrepair and, from the reluctance of Fountains Abbey to accept any

*Bradley Grange Farm in the 1980s. It was formerly thought to be the site of the grange for Fountains Abbey but that is likely to have been at Bradley Hall.* G Redmonds

responsibility for this vital link with the Bradley property, we can only infer that its importance had declined considerably. Perhaps the ironstone deposits were already worked out or uneconomic to extract.

The monks' problems at Bradley, as elsewhere in their dependencies, were inevitably made worse by the plague of 1349-50 and, in 1363, the abbot of Fountains wrote a petition in which he described the Bradley estate as ruinous, the buildings broken down and the lands reduced almost to sterility. It seems likely that the grange was now considered to be a burden to the abbey and it was proposed to overcome this by converting it into a manor run by a secular landlord. From the fragmentary records of the next one hundred years or so we can infer that this was done and that it was held by the Greenwoods and the Snaiths, although we know little about these families. However, in 1478 it passed into the hands of the Pilkingtons who were its landlords until the Dissolution and long after.

During their occupation the former grange came to be known as Bradley Hall, and a derelict farm with this name survives on the site, still linked to other parts of the estate by the old highway called Steep Lane.[92] The Pilkington family finally sold their Bradley estate in 1829, but the hall's decline may have started as early as the 1600s, after they had moved to Chevet, and it is only recently that the importance of the site has been recognised. The identification was made more difficult because the name Bradley Grange had been given to the more recent Grange Farm. The difficulties which arose when these former monastic granges were forfeited to the Crown emerge in a fascinating tithe case of the 1540s which, in some respects, echoes those of former centuries.[93]

## Dispute at Bradley

There were two issues in this case and the first related to the payment of tithes in money and not in kind. The second, though, had to do with the status of Bradley before and after the Dissolution for, although much of it had belonged to Fountains Abbey, it still formed part of Huddersfield parish. A further complication arose because the parish church was formerly appropriated to the monastery of St Oswald and had, therefore, passed to the Crown. The tithes had been leased to the Pilkingtons by St Oswald's, first on a 40-year lease and then on a 23-year lease, the annual payment changing from 8s to 16s 8d. The parties involved were the prosecutor, John Thornell or Thornhill of Fixby, acting as the guardian of Nicholas and Thomas Thornhill who were minors, and the defendants, local yeoman

*The ruins of Bradley Hall Farm. This was probably the site of the abbey grange.*
Tony Burke

families such as the Brooks, Gibsons and Hirsts. It is worth noting that in the depositions the estate was described as 'the manor or grange called Bradley Moor or Bradley Grange', but that tenants referred to it as Bradley Hall.

Soon after the manor had changed hands, a number of Bradley tenants were accused of failing to pay their tithes and several of them had to appear at the Consistory Court of the Archbishop at York. Christopher Brook, for example, was said 'to have harvested ten wain loads of hay, valued at 6s a load', which he had converted to his own use and for which he refused to pay tithe. He disputed these accusations, asserting that his hay harvest was less than they were claiming and that the local price for hay was 3s 4d a cart load, not 6s as they maintained. Moreover, he said, he was 'never demaunded by any person to pay any tieth of his haye'.

Similar evidence was offered by Thomas Hyrst and Thomas Gibson. The latter's statement may not have been the neatest form of words possible but its message was clear; he 'hathe not had never a yere hiderto not past oone loode and an halfe'. Christopher's claim had been that nobody had asked him to pay, but Thomas Brook's defence was that he had 'paid his tieth for his porcion unto Bradley Hall', and was not obliged to 'paie any tiethe to any oodre personne but to the hed manor'. In fact, there seems to have been some doubt in everybody's mind about the customs relating to the Bradley tithe, for witnesses were also asked 'wyther they have knowne or hard saye that the tith corne, hay or other tithes off Bradley... have beyn usyd to be payd in money or how myche money was payd... yerly'.

Doubtless, part of the 'bewilderment' expressed by the Bradley tenants during their interrogation was for the benefit of the court, but it is clear from the proceedings that the whole matter had become very complicated. Thomas and Nicholas Thornhill 'were in possession of the tithes by the receipt of a pension or rent of the tithes – paid by the hands of Arthur Pilkington', but the tithes themselves, and the lands on which they were calculated, had by then passed to the Crown. In 1544 the Crown had sold the tithes to Richard Andrews and William Ramsden of Longley, and the latter was doubtless acting as an agent for the Thornhills, to whom 'all the said tithes' were granted in the same year.

*Much of the fabric of Bradley Hall is relatively recent but this old doorway dates from the seventeenth century.* Tony Burke

It is hardly surprising that problems arose as a result of such transactions, nor that the new landlords should find themselves in dispute with local farmers. Nor should we be surprised that the case went against the defendants, although those at the lower end of the social scale were not the only ones to meet with difficulties. Indeed, for William Ramsden of Longley the consequences of his speculation in monastic property were to last throughout his life! His first purchase in the early 1540s had not been made direct from the Crown, but through the offices of two large-scale speculators, Andrews and Chamberlain. He was a shrewd enough man to realise how profits could be made as an agent and this probably explains how he came to be associated with Andrews in the Bradley deal. Unfortunately, it seems that not all the men he represented were able to find the sums they needed, and it was not long before William Ramsden found himself in the debtors' prison known as the Fleet – an experience he was to go through more than once in the years that followed.[94]

### Settlements in Bradley

The evidence suggests that Bradley's population in the sixteenth and seventeenth centuries may have been restricted to no more than half a dozen families, and the first to expand there were the Hirsts, Brooks and Gibsons. None of these had origins in Bradley, although the Hirsts and Brooks had both been prominent in Huddersfield from the late 1200s and the Gibsons came from Southowram, where Richard, son of Gilbert (1354) seems to have been the progenitor.[95] Other families to move into the district in the 1600s were the Mallinsons, Amblers, Kayes and Sheards, again all from townships close by.

Apart from the Hall or former Grange we can identify just six or seven houses in Bradley in this period, the earliest being Bradley Gate, near Newhouse in Deighton, Lodge and Fell Greave, all recorded before 1560. The Oak, Lamb Cote and Shepherd's Thorn are referred to soon after that and there was a family named Hirst at Colne Bridge from at least the 1630s. These were all scattered dwellings, although Colne Bridge eventually became a focus for further settlement, some of it across the river in Kirkheaton parish. It was the nearest Bradley came to having a village nucleus and, ironically, it reflected the wider land interests that Fountains Abbey had once had. A brief account of one or two houses in this area may serve to illustrate what was happening in Bradley more generally.

*Bradley Bar, 1930, just before a major widening of the road.* Courtesy of the *Huddersfield Examiner*

*The Oak, a house built in 1751 by John Brooke, on the site of a much older settlement.* Courtesy of the *Huddersfield Examiner*

**Shepherd's Thorn**

Shepherd's Thorn lies to the east of an ancient lane running north from Sheepridge to Rastrick and Bradford. It was once a secluded farm but this has changed in recent years with the building of the M62 and the conversion of Bradley Park into a golf course. The documented history of the hamlet goes back well over four hundred years and the two main families associated with it up to 1600 were the Brooks and the Hirsts. Not very far away was Lamb Cote, the home of the Gibsons, now demolished.

One of the most misleading pieces of information concerning Shepherd's Thorn is the entry in A H Smith's *Place-Names of the West Riding* which cites two documents dated 1479 and 1481 relating to a case of trespass brought by the Prior of Monk Bretton. His complaint was that two men had 'seized and unjustly detained 360 sheep belonging to the priory at the place called Shepherd Thorn'. Unfortunately, this cannot be Shepherd's Thorn in Bradley, for both documents make it quite clear that the locality in question was part of either Notton or Darton, both of which are in the Barnsley area. Nevertheless, the document mentioned may indirectly throw some light on the Bradley place-name. We know, for example, that when Bradley declined and proved unprofitable the abbey allowed the estate to pass into secular hands. Although their main interest and the major source of their profit was the production of iron, there is no

*Throstle Nest, a cottage at the side of the old highway between Shepherd's Thorn and Toothill, now demolished.* G Redmonds collection

doubt, also, that they kept significant flocks of sheep there. As early as 1194-98 a grant to the monks provided for pasture in Bradley for 180 sheep and lambs and it is possible that the area given over to sheep pasture increased when the estate passed into the hands of lay tenants. That would certainly help to explain the adjoining place-names Shepherd's Thorn and Lamb Cote.

Although much of the history of these hamlets is still obscure, we know that the Brooks and Gibsons who lived there in the mid-1500s were clothiers and that the farms remained part of the Pilkington's Bradley estate until its sale in 1829.[96] It is the sales catalogue of that year which gives us another illuminating glimpse into their history. Shepherd's Thorn consisted then of two groups of farm-buildings tenanted by Robert Smith and Jonas Heywood. Robert Smith paid £66 rent per year for forty acres which lay mostly to the north and east. Jonas Heywood had fifty-seven acres at a rent of £93 10s which stretched south to the Dewsbury and Elland turnpike. The two farms at Lamb Cote were tenanted by members of the Schofield and Ibbotson families and amounted to something over twenty-four acres at £40 rent.

As a final comment, it is interesting to note that no fewer than six of the fields at Shepherd's Thorn incorporated the name Savile. This famous Yorkshire family first came into the Bradley story when Nicholas Savile was granted custody of Robert Pilkington's son Arthur in 1497. Arthur later married Alice Savile and a Bryan Savile died at Shepherd's Thorn in 1606.

### Padanaram (Colne Bridge)

Most people who drive from Waterloo to Colne Bridge do not go via the town centre but take the more direct route through Dalton. For the last part of this journey the road which runs close to the River Colne is actually in Kirkheaton, although now it seems quite remote from the church and the village. As early as the twelfth century much of this riverside land, called Colne Bottoms, was granted to Fountains Abbey by local landowners, who gave permission for them to build a mill and dam there. In more recent times, from 1792 to 1802, it was the site of an iron forge operated by Samuel Day.[97]

On the face of it the area had many advantages: Colne Bridge and Cooper Bridge gave access to the Calder Valley and the important routes north and south; the river provided power for the early mills and the land was easily converted into good pastures and meadow. Now, of course, very little of this land lies on the Kirkheaton side of the river, but there have been so many alterations in its course over

*Padanaram, near Colne Bridge, built for William Brook, 1776-78.* Tony Burke

the centuries, both natural and man-made, that it would be unwise to presume that this was always the case. Unfortunately, the fast-flowing river could also be a great disadvantage and floods were a constant threat, damaging the land and mills and frequently sweeping away the wooden bridges. In 1617, for example, it was ordered in Kirkheaton court rolls that 'the Ruyns of a close called Colnebottome' should be repaired by those who had failed to secure the river defences,[98] while an estate survey of 1813 stated simply that Samuel Day's premises were liable to be flooded.[99] The iron-works across the river fared even worse, and a disastrous flood in 1706 not only took 'a great part of the Charcoale Stock away', but left 'the Remainder in a verry bad Condition'.[100]

One of the most interesting houses in this part of Kirkheaton is the old farm with the unusual name Padanaram, which appears on Jeffreys's map of 1771-72 as Pading Narvin. However, the present building was probably put up in 1776-78, for it is mentioned in the accounts of the Whitley Beaumont Estate.[101] The builder was Benjamin Berry, the carpenter George Redfearn and the plasterer David Tunnacliffe, and all these men were regularly employed on estate building projects. Their combined bills amounted to £70 14s 9d, a modest sum by modern standards. Although it is not yet certain who the first occupant of the farm was, the accounts show that the tenant in 1776 was called William Brook and there are several intriguing references to his property in the months following the completion of the building. One of these suggests that woodland in the vicinity was still being used to provide charcoal, for William Wilcock was paid for 'valueing wood in padan Aram' in 1777-78, whilst in the following year over £30 was paid for stone needed for building a weir there, most of which was provided by Abraham Graham. It is difficult to know exactly what function this weir served but, as it was sometimes referred to as a 'west wall', it is probable that it was simply a strengthening of the banks to prevent flooding.

The estate surveys of 1793 and 1813 provide further interesting details. On both occasions Thomas Barlow was the tenant and his premises were described as a slate-roofed, stone building with two rooms downstairs and two bedrooms. There was also a good cellar and an old stone barn detached, surviving probably from an older house on the site. All these were 'in tolerable repair'.[102] One of the fields attached to the farm was Allott Royd, a riverside clearance going back in all probability to the thirteenth century.

Padanaram may seem an unusual name for a local farm, but it was no doubt familiar to our ancestors from the reference in the book of Genesis to Isaac, who married 'the daughter of Bethuel the Syrian, of Padan-aram'. Biblical names for late settlements were not at all uncommon and there is a Mount Pisgah in the same parish and at least one other Padanaram locally, near Stainland. It may, however, be more subtle than that, and Professor Dickins has suggested that as it means in Hebrew 'tilled land of the highlands', it may be a case of someone showing off his knowledge of the language.

### Heaton Lodge (Colne Bridge)

A few hundred yards from Colne Bridge, half-hidden by trees, stands Heaton Lodge, derelict in the 1980s but now happily restored to something of its former grandeur. The extent of its decline in those years becomes apparent when we examine an estate survey of 1813 which described the building in detail.[103] It allows us to visualise the ground floor with its dining-room, vestibule and central staircase. Something of a surprise to us now are the bedrooms at each end with

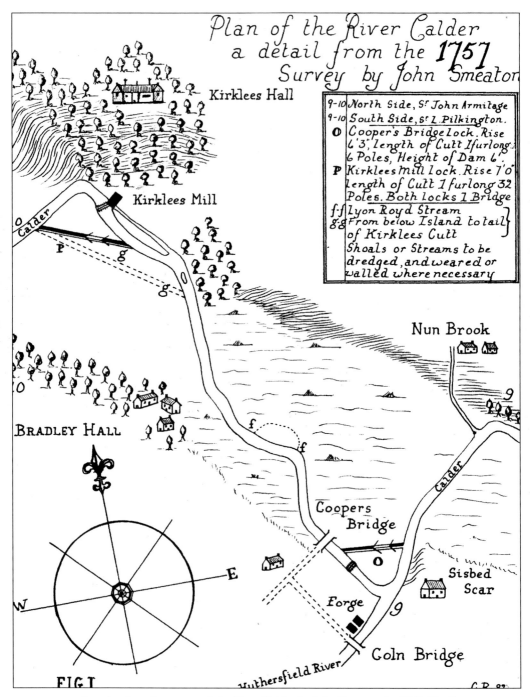

*Plan of the River Calder a detail from the* **1757** *Survey by John Smeaton*

| 9-10 | North Side, Sʳ John Armitage |
|---|---|
| 9-10 | South Side, Sʳ L Pilkington. |
| O | Cooper's Bridge Lock. Rise 6'3", length of Cutt 1 furlong. 6 Poles, Height of Dam 6'. |
| P | Kirklees Mill lock. Rise 7'0" length of Cutt 1 furlong 32 Poles. Both locks 1 Bridge |
| f-f | lyon Royd Stream |
| g-g | From below Island to tail } of Kirklees Cutt Shoals or Streams to be dredged, and weared or walled where necessary |

Kirklees Hall

Kirklees Mill

Calder

Nun Brook

BRADLEY HALL

Coopers Bridge

Sisbed Scar

Forge

Coln Bridge

Huthersfield River

FIG I

*A section from the survey of the River Calder by John Smeaton in 1757. Bradley Hall and the Colne Bridge Forge are clearly shown.* G Redmonds collection

*Heaton Lodge, Colne Bridge, 1988.* Courtesy of the *Huddersfield Examiner*

their own dressing-rooms, but that was certainly the arrangement, and this floor probably formed the family's main living space. Upstairs, for example, were a shoe-room, a laundry and no fewer than seven 'lodging-rooms', two of them again with dressing-rooms. This number suggests that the family often had guests but the details of their entertainment at the Lodge have to be left to the imagination.

The basement, as one might expect, was the domain of the domestic staff, with its pantry, kitchen, shoe-room and larder; there was also a servants' hall and special accommodation for the butler and the house-keeper. Equally comprehensive was the range of outbuildings to the south of the house, with stabling and sixteen 'Halls with good granaries'. Across the courtyard were a detached dairy and larder, a saddle-room, scullery and 'sundry offices'. The farm buildings were grouped round the upper fold; there were cow-houses, pig-cotes, more stables, this time probably for the working horses, and hay chambers. Specialist buildings included a coach-house, a detached pigeon-house and shops or work places for a butcher and a blacksmith. These all point to the self-sufficiency of the estate, and one final entry, 'the fireplaces for the excellent range of Hothouses', completes this picture of a fine Georgian residence in a landscape of woods and well-cared-for gardens.

The name Heaton Lodge seems to have been coined with the intention of giving the new house a touch of class, possibly inviting people to link it with Heaton Hall a couple of hundred yards up the road. Historically, lodges were more modest dwellings, set within a deer park and providing a home for the park's keeper, but the term was acquiring much grander status about this time, perhaps through association with the shooting parties which were becoming so popular with the gentry. Heaton Lodge had no connection with the farm called Lodge, which occupied a traditional site within Bradley Park, just across the river.

The position of the house, in the years before the worst effects of the Industrial Revolution took their toll, must have been magnificent. When it was put up for lease in 1820 it was described as 'situate on an eminence near the River Calder, commanding a very beautiful and extensive prospect over a highly picturesque country'.[104] These are almost exactly the words used by the surveyor of the estate seven years earlier. Other advertised advantages of the 'modern-built Mansion' were its proximity to the important Leeds-Huddersfield Road and seventy-five acres of land, meadow and pasture.

The house belonged to the Beaumonts of Whitley Hall and it was leased by them to George Bernard who, in 1774, had married Elizabeth the sister of Richard Henry Beaumont. This lease contains several interesting bits of information, for it was dated 27 March 1793 and referred to 'the Mansion House now erecting by George Bernard... late Lieutenant-Colonel of His Majesty's 86th Regiment of Foot'.[105] He was later to become General Bernard and his connections, if not always his behaviour, were impeccable. According to the Kirkheaton historian Legh Tolson he was related to Admiral Codrington, who commanded the Orion at Trafalgar and he was himself Usher of the Black Rod during the Vice-Royalty of the Duke of Rutland in Ireland. The couple had no children but George Bernard was apparently father to an illegitimate daughter, first known simply as Fanny Grey, who took her father's name and arms in 1819. The mother was Elizabeth Proctor of Bayard's Lodge, near Knaresborough.

Although we have no full biography of the Bernards, there are several intriguing references to them in local documents. Mrs Bernard said in a letter to her brother in 1791, 'Mother is something better but still extraordinarily weak and low. She begs to see You', and then, 'if you dine here there's nothing to offer but a beefsteak which was ordered for Colonel Bernard'.[106] Presumably her husband was unexpectedly away from home. An enigmatic note in the letter, which may have had something to do with events described later, reads 'mother would prefer you to come alone without brother John and his son'. Another letter in May 1792 refers to the receipt of a box of jewels by Mrs Bernard, returned by William Fenton of Spring Grove.[107] There must have been some family argument over these, for John Beaumont, her brother, afterwards referred to the Bernards' possession of the jewels, which, he said, had belonged to his 'late mother and which she had never given to them' (i.e. the Bernards). This affair may have had something to do with the fact that John had an heir while his sister was childless.

Two incidents in 1802 seem to have threatened the even tenor of life at Heaton Lodge. It was the Honley historian Alan Brooke who drew our attention to a letter received in August of that year by General Bernard, which demanded that the store of arms at the house should be removed and left in a field for collection. The writer, who represented a militant group of workers in the neighbourhood, said that failure to comply with this order would result in the house being blown up, but apparently nothing came of the threat.[108] In the same year the General seems also to have been involved in a dispute over the iron-forge operated by Samuel Day at Colne Bridge. His butler, Johnson, attended talks about the closure of the forge which had something to do with smoke and the slitting-mill.[109] If this was an early case of pollution in the Colne Valley, the matter was soon resolved, for the Beaumonts, who were the owners, obliged Day to close down the works and remove the steam engine.

With the death of Mrs Bernard in 1814 and that of her husband six years afterwards, this phase of the history of Heaton Lodge came to an end. Later, it was tenanted by Jonathan Haigh, a cotton-spinner, and then apparently became a boys' boarding-school under Messrs Fairweather and Bishop. The story of those years and the house's subsequent decline and restoration is still waiting to be told.

### Colne Bridge Mills

The cotton mills at Colne Bridge, which occupied the site of the former iron forge, encountered a variety of problems in the early years of the nineteenth century, not to mention the dreadful tragedy which cost seventeen girls their lives. At different times the mills had been run by the Rawstornes and then the Atkinsons,[110] but in the early 1830s, when a dispute sprang up over the canal, Thomas Haigh was the tenant. His correspondence for those years is particularly interesting.[111] It was his view that the Colne Bridge Mills, which were on the Pilkingtons estate, could no longer operate profitably, largely because of the way the Ramsden Canal was being used. One complaint concerned the direct flow of water in the River Colne. Normally, the supply would have been sufficient to power the waterwheel at Colne Bridge, even in the summer season, but Haigh claimed that this was no longer so.

The tenants of mills in Huddersfield, he said, ran the water off into their reservoirs or dams once they had finished work in the evening, and in consequence the night stream was reduced almost to nothing. However, the Ramsdens' mill at Shorefoot was working throughout the night, and to be able to do so, supplied itself with water from the basin of the canal and that portion of it which extended to Red Doles Lock. Frequently, therefore, in the morning, the canal was so drained

*This stone is located inside the former mill buildings at Colne Bridge. It bears the date 1708 and commemorates work carried out at the iron forge, listing the parties involved.* Courtesy of the *Huddersfield Examiner*

*The lock at Cooper Bridge.* Tony Burke

that it was not navigable until 10 or 11 o'clock, during which period the water which should have flowed down the Colne was diverted into the canal to make good the deficiency. Moreover, by this time, the mills upstream were also working, all of which was to the great disadvantage of Thomas Haigh's mill. 'It is no uncommon thing', he wrote, 'for the mill, or part of it, to be standing for three or four hours together for want of water, and the work people playing half the forenoon'.

A second complaint concerned the canal users. Thomas Haigh asserted that on occasion it was now being navigated by vessels carrying from forty to fifty tons, twice what had originally been intended. His argument is worth quoting in full:

*Now, when a heavily loaded vessel enters the Canal at Cooper Bridge Lock, in order to float her they are obliged to supply water from the pond above, in such quantity as will raise the pond below three or four inches above the level of the lock gates; the necessary consequence is that it flows over the top of the gates at Cooper Bridge in a stream three or four inches deep. And on the other hand when a vessel fully loaded up with wool goes up the canal, from the bulk of the article and the lowness of the canal bridges, it not infrequently happens that they are compelled to let a great quantity of water out of the canal so as to reduce its level...and enable the vessel to pass under the bridges.*

This meant, of course, if it were true, that Haigh's mill suffered another serious loss of water; a remedy, he said, was becoming daily a matter of greater necessity. There can be no doubt, I think, that his claim had some substance. It would be tedious here to quote at length from all the correspondence but, in January 1833, Bradley Clay admitted to Haigh that 'some person unknown had drawn some of the pools below Red Doles Lock', and later the same year he confirmed that he had given instructions 'to fine every one who draws off the water illegally'.

The episode is of particular interest in that it illustrates the interdependence of the two waterways, canal and river. The volume of available water was no greater than in the past, but the amount of work it was being called on to perform had certainly increased.

# 6 *A*LMONDBURY

## Castle Hill

*I think the fault of our town has been that too little attention has been paid to its ornamentation – I mean its ornamentation apart from mere utility. Huddersfield, with its widely extended municipal boundary, has a feature within its borders which I believe to be unique. I know of no city or borough in the kingdom with an elevation 900 feet above sea-level such as we have in Castle Hill... I do not know which is the better – the view of the surrounding country from Castle Hill, or the view of the hill itself from the numberless points whence it can be seen... suffice it to say that a view extending from Skelmanthorpe on one side, to the Lancashire Hills on the other, from the heights beyond Bradford on the north, to the Derbyshire Hills on the south – a view so extensive is no common one, and the elevation might fitly be emphasised by erecting upon it a suitable tower, which would challenge observation from an area of 300 square miles, and this I would call the 'Victoria Tower'.* G W Tomlinson

(From a letter to the editor of the *Huddersfield Daily Chronicle*, 4 Feb. 1897)[112]

Castle Hill, probably more than any other place locally, has the power to stimulate our imagination, for it rises high above the town and its distinctive contours bear enigmatic traces of ancient earthworks. It was here that men settled over 4,000 years ago and here too that a catastrophic fire later destroyed the great iron age fort. A Norman castle was also built on the hill, in King Stephen's time, and then demolished after an abortive rebellion by the Earl of Lancaster; some of the debris was thrown down the well and the rest piled up in a great mound.[113] It is that ruined castle which explains the name we now use for the hill, despite the vestigial nature of the remains, but there are other names associated with the hill's past that have more power to appeal to our imagination.

The oldest of these may be preserved in 'Cater Croft' and 'Catterstones', two names that are first recorded in the sixteenth and seventeenth centuries. 'Croft' and 'stones' require no explanation; they referred to a field and to a stony area of common land close to the hill, and were simple enough additions to the much older 'cater'. This Celtic word for a hill or hill fort is an element found in other

*A view of Catterstones from Castle Hill.* G Redmonds

ancient place-names, such as Catterton near Tadcaster, or Cader Idris the name of a Welsh mountain, and it is preserved today in Catterstones, the name of the farm just below the summit of the hill.

The hill fort is said to have been abandoned about 430 BC but place-names tell us that the British continued to live in the area, so stories about the disaster that had overtaken the fort may have lived on. However, it seems unlikely that these could have been shared with the Anglians and Danes who later settled near by, although the hill's threatening presence may have caused them equal apprehension. We shall never know what the hill meant to any of these people but they could hardly have ignored it. Even if no such folk stories survived new tales of horror kindled superstition and dread when the Norman castle dominated the skyline. Hulbert, for example, relates a story of cruelties committed in the dungeons of the castle, of a stranger in disguise who was slain there and his body eaten by birds and dogs.[114]

It is against this background that we should seek to understand the

*The Victoria Tower on Castle Hill, built by public subscription in 1899.* Courtesy of the *Huddersfield Examiner*

place-name Wormcliffe, obscure no doubt to most local people, but familiar to those who have studied Almondbury's earliest manorial documents. It first occurs in a rental of 1425, in the phrase 'three acres of demesne land called Wormcliffe – where the castle used to stand', and this wording occurs again in a manorial survey of 1584.[115] In the Ministers' Accounts of 1487, it was more precisely identified as 'the castle of Wornecliff'.

The 'cliff' was almost certainly the hill itself, but the word 'worm' is particularly suggestive, for it was used by our ancestors to describe a serpent, or any fearful creature that might haunt old ruins or guard hidden treasure. The word 'drake' for dragon was used in a similar way and it is not unusual to find ancient burial mounds given such names as Wormlaw or Drakehowe. The suspicion must be that people were overawed by the ruins and ancient earthworks and saw the looming hill as a place of dread. What we don't know is exactly when the place-name was coined, and that is tantalising. Speaking of Wormcliffe the survey of 1584 says that it was 'never known to any person within the memory of man where the same do lie', making it clear that it was all to do with the ancient past. Just how ancient the story of a resident serpent might be we shall never know.[116]

## Almondbury beacon
There was a beacon on Castle Hill for centuries, but it never gave its name to the hill as some beacons did, and there are relatively few early references to it, although it is thought that one was first erected late in Elizabeth's reign, when Spain threatened invasion. Almondbury's beacon was part of a chain designed to pass the warning from hill-top to hill-top and its immediate neighbours were at High Hoyland, Southowram and Revey Hill in North Bierley.[117] In fact it was to commemorate the 400th anniversary of the ill-fated Spanish Armada that the present replica beacon was set up in 1988.

The first real evidence we have for the beacon on Castle Hill is the estate map of 1634 which shows it as an iron basket at the top of a long pole. The pole had supporting struts and there seem to have been handles set into it so that the watchmen might climb up and load the basket with fuel. It is in the Quarter Sessions Order books that we find references to these beacons, usually at a time when danger threatened, and this happened in 1666 at the time of the Dutch War. Thomas Starkye was the Almondbury constable that year and he claimed expenses of £3 1s 2d for supplying 'combustible material' to the beacon and keeping watch. The magistrates ordered that 'an estreate bee forthwith made for the same on Agbrigg and

*The replica beacon, erected in 1988.* G Redmonds

Morley Wapentake',[118] and the township books of some neighbouring villages confirm that the cost was shared.

It is most unlikely that a watch was maintained on the hill throughout periods of peace and the beacons were either vandalised or fell into disrepair very quickly. However, each national emergency would require them to be returned to a state of readiness and this happened in 1685 when James II was the king, an avowed Catholic on the throne of a Protestant kingdom. There were two major alarms, the first an abortive invasion in May by the ninth Earl of Argyll and the second in June, when the Duke of Monmouth landed at Lyme Regis and raised an army of sorts. He was finally defeated at Sedgemoor on 5 July, but for a time there had been real anxiety.

Joseph Whitehead was the Almondbury constable on that occasion and there are two documents which relate to the beacon when he was in office. The first was a request in 1685 for expenses, and payment of these was duly authorised by the magistrates. The bill for £2 19s 6d has survived:

| | |
|---|---|
| *Paid to Jo. Freatwill for wood for the becin* | *15s 0d* |
| *Paid to Adam Beaumont for woork about the becon* | *16s 4d* |
| *Paid Jo. Booth for the brandrills mending* | *2s 0d* |
| *Paid a draight leadeing wood two days* | *8s 0d* |
| *Paid to Thos. Ralison for drenk* | *10s 6d* |
| *Paid to John North for bread* | *1s 0d* |
| *And for two men and towe horses Monday* | *2s 8d* |
| *And for all myn own laber about it and for comeing to the Sesons* | *4s 0d* [119] |

The second was a petition in 1686 after he had ceased to be constable, made necessary, it seems, because he had later had to erect a new beacon, 'the old one being formerly blown downe and totally decayed'. The expenses on this occasion amounted to £3 13s 4d and they were again 'estreated' on the Wapentake. Finally, in 1702, just two months after Queen Anne had come to the throne, and England was again at war with the French, it was ordered at the Sessions 'that £12 be estreated on Agbrigg and Morley and paid to Robert Reed, constable of Almondbury, for repairing and building the beacon at Almondbury'.

## The Failed Borough
There is a narrow footpath which leaves Sharp Lane in Almondbury and then runs roughly parallel to Westgate before joining the lane to Grasscroft. To the south of the path, a number of narrow uniform fields run down the hill in parallel lines; to the north an interesting pattern of housing fronts onto Westgate. This has already been commented on by J E Taylor, who drew attention to the concentration of buildings along the street, amounting to no fewer than two hundred dwellings, which lie alongside 'several short roads or folds' at right angles to the street.[120] This arrangement can be seen to have its origins in the crofts and houses depicted on Senior's 1634 map of the township.[121]

These features may be all that remains in Almondbury of an experiment in commercial development begun some seven hundred years ago. The village stood then at the junction of important highways which linked the valleys of the Holme and Colne with places of greater importance to the south and east. It had been granted a weekly market in 1294 and a three-day annual fair – a clear attempt to stimulate commercial activity. Less well documented is the

*Stiles on the old footpath that runs behind the crofts of the houses in Westgate, Almondbury.* Courtesy of the *Huddersfield Examiner*

*The long crofts in Almondbury that run downhill, parallel to Sharp Lane, possibly extensions of the original burgage crofts.* Clifford Stephenson

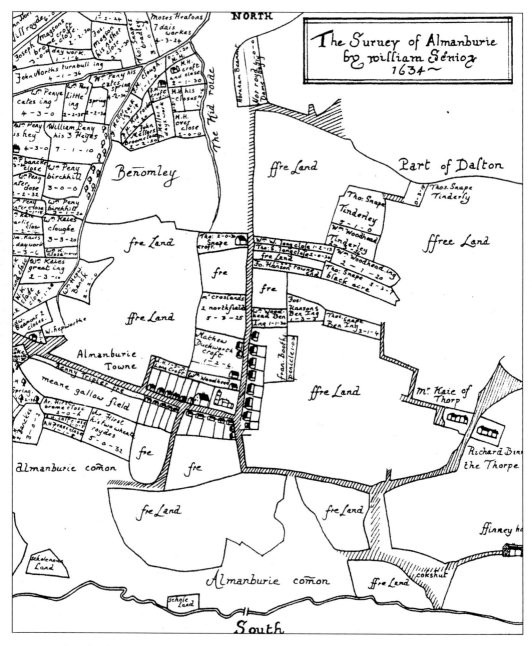

*A section from the survey of Almondbury by William Senior, in 1634, showing the houses and crofts on Westgate.* G Redmonds collection

*This aerial view of Castle Hill shows the Victoria Tower, the Castle Hill Hotel and the rough outline of the much earlier hill fort.* Clifford Stephenson

attempt at roughly the same time to give Almondbury borough status, although place-names, title deeds and aerial photographs point to such a development within the outer bailey on Castle Hill.

The uniform crofts on Westgate present the appearance of a planned landscape and seem likely to be connected with this venture, although it is not known whether they formed part of the original scheme, or whether failure at Castle Hill was followed by an attempt to focus activity on the village. That question is unlikely to be answered, but the evidence for the borough is clear enough and the Westgate crofts in particular have the appearance of 'burgage' tenancies. In order to encourage urban activity in the centuries after the Norman Conquest, tenants could be freed from the more onerous feudal obligations and be granted plots of land at fixed annual rents. These typical 'burgage' plots were long and narrow, with frontage on to a street or market area. The aim was to create conditions in which the tenants could carry on trades and crafts, forming an urban community.

The population growth of the thirteenth century and the agricultural expansion which accompanied it help to explain such attempts at urbanisation but, as we now know, the plagues of the fourteenth century caused many such experiments to fail and this may be what happened in Almondbury. Although 'burgage' plots were still being mentioned in Almondbury title deeds as late as the seventeenth century, the poll tax of 1379, with its details of residents and occupations, provides clear evidence that the 'borough' had come to nothing. Now only the landscape carries visible marks of the failed scheme, partly in the Westgate crofts and partly in the footpath which appears to define their limits. The surviving longer fields we see today may mark an early extension southwards, possibly given in compensation to those unfortunate early 'burgage' tenants.

One of the most interesting items on the 1634 map are the words 'scite of towne', written across the eastern half of Castle Hill, and these have been said to refer back to the burgage plots in the former outer bailey. Recently discovered deeds refer to 'a messuage or burgage scituate on the topp of the Castlehill... now being ruinated', suggesting that buildings survived as late as 1629.[122]

## Longley Old Hall

The present façade of Longley Old Hall is something of an enigma: its many interesting features include the mullioned windows set under label moulds, the massive pointed arch lintel of the doorway and the gabled roof with balled finials on the eaves. The apparent unity masks centuries of change, some of it visible and some discernible only to the experts. A recent report on the house said 'there is little to suggest that the stonework conceals the remains of three timber-framed ranges'.[123]

It has been said that in 1830 the house had two main gables and a central porch, which had probably changed little in two hundred or more years of history. Soon afterwards, however, these features were removed and that gave the house a much plainer appearance: a door in the north end and extra lights in the window above it, seen on a photograph of 1880, are signs that it may have been partitioned at the same time and adapted for use by hand-loom weavers. Its decline in status is explicit in G S Phillips's description of it as a 'poor and naked' cottage in 1848.

In 1884 Sir John Ramsden ordered the restoration of the hall and that decision no doubt owed something to fashion and something also to the importance he attached to it as the family's ancestral home. He went to considerable trouble to make it authentic both

*Longley Hall, just after its restoration in 1885.* Courtesy of Kirklees Cultural Services

inside and out: panelling and furniture were brought in from elsewhere, and gave the interior what Hulbert called 'a most quaint and pleasing appearance', whilst externally all traces of the earlier nineteenth-century alterations to windows and doors were removed. Having talked with old people who could remember the former hall Hulbert was confident that the addition of gables and finials had restored its original appearance.

Ironically, the Ramsdens' links with the old hall are far more tenuous than is generally realised. It is unlikely that William Ramsden acquired possession of it from his brother-in-law Thomas Savile before 1540 and by 1576, as his own records show, a start had been made on the new hall at Nether Longley. He almost certainly carried out major alterations to the old house in that period but the only information relating to those years is a memorandum of 1544 that 'foure tymber trees... toward the reparacion of his house at Longley' were obtained from woods at Bramley.[124]

As Dennis Whomsley has shown, William Ramsden passed a

limited amount of time at the hall in the period 1544-76. He spent almost two years in the Fleet prison for debt and on release in 1559 separated from his wife Joan, who continued to live at Longley Hall. William, however, moved restlessly around the kingdom, enduring at least one more period of imprisonment before his death in London in 1580, at the age of sixty-seven. It should also be remembered that after a period at their new hall in Longley the Ramsdens left the district for Byram in the 1600s, after which they administered their Huddersfield and Almondbury properties from a distance.

## Obscure Immigrant

When an unusual name occurs in local records it is tempting to try to find out what we can about the person behind the name. In this case the unusual name is Renatus or Rene Trippier and on 6 December 1629 this man married Susan Harpin at Almondbury parish church. The Harpin family had been established in the neighbourhood for generations but there is no doubt that Susan's husband was a newcomer to the village, probably a Frenchman. It is true that Renatus, meaning 'reborn', was used occasionally by English Puritans in the early 1600s, but it was more popular in

*Almondbury parish church in the early 1900s.* G Redmonds collection

France, and Trippier was certainly French – the occupational term for a dealer in tripe. One possibility is that Rene Trippier was a Protestant, fleeing from France to avoid religious persecution. Just two years earlier the important French stronghold at La Rochelle had revolted against the King and sought help from England, but they were defeated in 1629 and deprived of the privileges gained at the Edict of Nantes. The Almondbury vicar at the time certainly had Puritan leanings, for his nephew bore the innovative christian name Whatgodwill.

Many of those who fled France were influential tradesmen and we know that Rene Trippier became a 'mercer' in Almondbury. It is not always clear just what a mercer's stock in trade was but Rene was selling tobacco in 1632, so he may have dealt in a variety of small goods in addition to textile fabrics. From the parish register we know that he lived in the village rather than in one of the outlying hamlets, and his distinctive name is on the map of 1634, as the free tenant of a strip of land alongside Kaye Lane. It lay on the south side of the highway, between what are now Wheatroyd Lane and Sharp Lane, and he had acquired it in 1632 from John Kaye of Thorpe. There is a puzzling item in a rental of this man's property in 1634, which lists Rene's house and shop and refers to him as the son of John Kaye.[125] Other evidence points to a close connection between Rene Trippier and the Kayes, so it may be that he was the son-in-law and that Susan Harpin had been a widow when she married him.

We also know a good deal about this man's family, although some details are quite likely to be missing from the Almondbury Registers. The first of several daughters was Mary, born in 1632, but she died twelve months later; as he gave the same name to a second daughter in 1639 it may be that Mary had special associations for him back in France. Grace, who was born in 1640, also failed to survive beyond her first year but Susan and Martha were more fortunate, the former eventually marrying a local man. Sara, and an only son Rene, both died tragically when they were eighteen. Rene the father died in 1658, fifteen years after his wife, and William Hepworth was the administrator of his goods.[126] However, Rene must have been married twice, for Mary, the mother of William Finnay of Almondbury, was said to be his wife in 1655[127] and a widow Trippier 'of town' was buried in 1659.

Several incidents in Rene's life are preserved in the court rolls and Quarter Sessions. We know that he was elected constable in 1652 and then fined 13s 4d for refusing to serve in that office, and he was involved, also, in several cases of felony. He was the victim in 1656,

*Several houses on Westgate in Almondbury preserve ancient features but Wormall Hall, directly opposite the church, is probably the oldest, much older than 1631, the date carved on the lintel.* G Redmonds

when 'one secke of unwynnowed oates' valued at 4s was stolen from him, but on two other occasions he was accused of theft himself – once in 1653 for stealing a duck from George Wilkinson, to which he pleaded 'not guilty', and once in 1639 for stealing a pound of tobacco from Thomas Brooke, valued at 6s – to which he confessed. What is curious is the omission of Rene's name from the Almondbury Oath of Protestation in 1642, for he was certainly living in the village at that time. As a foreigner he may have been excused or not required to sign.

It is unlikely that Rene was survived by any male descendants but the surname did not die out. In 1642 a David Trippier was living in Lockwood and must have been over eighteen to have taken the oath. He could have been the younger brother of Rene and this seems even more likely when we discover that he called his son Rene in 1651. There are no more references to the family after 1679, when Dorothy Trippier of Lockwood was buried, but David's death is not recorded and he may simply have moved out of the parish. That possibility seems more likely when we read in the Quarter Sessions for 1732 that James Tripear was to be removed to Huddersfield from Langfield in Heptonstall chapelry: his children's names were Martha, David and John.[128]

## Squirrel Ditch

There are many corners of Huddersfield which remind us of its recent rural past and one of these is the evocatively named Squirrel Ditch. It can be reached via Newsome Road and was a local beauty spot in the nineteenth century, although it is unknown to a surprising number of present-day Huddersfield residents. According to G S Phillips, the scenery was wild and romantic there in the 1840s,[129] and an old photograph shows a pony and trap passing along a lane in a predominately wooded landscape, with hedges on either side, an old raised causeway, and a single dwelling.

A later reminiscence by John Sugden, written in affectionate terms, evokes the atmosphere of Squirrel Ditch in the 1920s, hidden in the

*Old cottages at Squirrel Ditch, at the junction with the former Cocker Lane.*
G Redmonds

picturesque woodland which had been laid out by the Ramsdens and was then in the care of Colonel Beadon. John Sugden was recalling that his father, a designer at Beaumont Taylor's in Moldgreen, had lodged there as a young man with a family called Dyson. Even now, no great effort of the imagination is required to see that this was once a most attractive hamlet, close to the town centre and to the King's Mill, not vastly different from many other small weaving communities in the area.

Confirmation that Squirrel Ditch was in fact such a community can be found in the census returns of 1851. The ten families living there were mostly involved in textiles, with one clothier, Ben Wray, and six weavers all with local names: Haigh (2), Blackburn, Sykes, Kaye and Wood. Samuel Whitley was a woollen spinner and Joseph Mitchell, a tailor. The only family not connected with the trade was that of Richard Jackson, a stone waller.

It was during the next twenty years that significant changes took place at Squirrel Ditch, although the total population showed only a slight increase. Nevertheless, at least one lady had moved there from Flintshire and two of the men came from Westmorland. Even local families came from places further afield; George Roberts, a fulling miller with eight children, was from Meltham, and his neighbours were from Kirkburton, Holmfirth and Wakefield. This greater diversity of origins is reflected in the occupations. There were still several families engaged in weaving but two men were goods porters and two were whitesmiths; there was a carpenter, two joiners and a leather dresser.

We assume, I think, that life moved at a much slower pace for our ancestors and that fundamental changes were fewer, but that can be misleading despite its general truth. The census returns have illustrated the important changes affecting the hamlet between 1851 and 1871, but it would be wrong to think that nothing much had disturbed the flow of life there previously. In fact estate maps and rentals paint a quite different picture. In 1634, for example, the map shows an area called the 'warrant' where Squirrel Ditch now is, that is land reserved for hunting small game, and it seems to have been completely uninhabited. It is difficult to say how old the place-name Squirrel Ditch might be, but it first appears in the rent book in 1780, as a cottage in the tenancy of John Cocker. It may be much older, since there had been Cockers on the rent roll since 1716, in an unnamed cottage. Cocker Lane was no doubt named after the family but that name has gone now, replaced by Wood Lane.

In fact, it is unlikely that there were woods in that area in 1634, and it is clear from later maps that the 'warrant' eventually gave way to fields. Many of these were still there in the mid-1800s, but some planting had taken place at Squirrel Ditch itself and Colonel Beadon was later responsible for the woods which cover the hillside now and help to give Squirrel Ditch its character. The growth of the hamlet itself was slow but it had begun by 1798, when Squirrel Ditch was represented by two names in the rental, those of John Cocker, possibly the man mentioned earlier or a near relative, and William North.

## Tunnacliffe Road

Many of our modern streets have a much longer history than we might suspect and some of them commemorate family connections that go back several hundred years. Tunnacliffe Road, in Newsome, is a good example, for its terrace houses are on the site of the former hamlet of Tunnacliffe Hill, named after a Newsome family. The

*The hamlet of Coldhill, on the flank of Castle Hill, 1983. The Blackburns were tenants here in the 1600s.* Courtesy of the *Huddersfield Examiner*

surname is still popular locally and it is usually spelt Tunnacliffe or, less commonly, Tunnicliffe. Both these derive from Tonacliffe, a locality in Rochdale parish, which is unusual in having three elements, i.e. 'town-well-cliff'. There was a family with this name in Rochdale from at least 1246, when Henry de Tunwaleclif was listed in a Lancashire assize roll, but the earliest Yorkshire reference goes back to 1397, when John de Thunwalclif witnessed a Meltham title deed.[130] He was one of several Saddleworth men to do so and, as Saddleworth was then in Rochdale parish, this might explain how Tunnacliffe found its way into the Huddersfield area.

In 1416 the surname is recorded in Thurstonland, in connection with iron working, and in 1445 Robin of Tonalclyf was living in Saddleworth.[131] These are scattered references, but interesting to local historians because Roche Abbey had property in both places and the connection may explain why members of the family moved into this part of Yorkshire. However, the first local Tunnacliffe who can be identified with any accuracy is John, a clothier in the Honley area in the 1530s and 1540s, who may be identical with a John Tonnycliff taxed under Crosland in 1524. He appears to be the only local man with the surname at that time, so it is not unreasonable to infer that it was one of his family who settled shortly afterwards in the area known as Newsome Wood. This place-name no longer exists but is used to describe an area of common land in Almondbury, on a slope facing north and west which was still largely undeveloped in the mid-1500s.

Thomas Tunnacliffe (although spellings such as Toonycliffe were more normal) was certainly a Newsome man. In the 1550s he was godfather to the children of several Newsome families, notably the Ratcliffes of Coldhill and the Dawsons of Newsome Wood.[132] He was himself said to be of Newsome Wood in 1570 and the manorial survey of 1584 confirms that he held 'one messuage, one barn, fold and garden' there, sharing the tenancy with a widow Dawson – possibly his mother-in-law. There is no map for this period to show us exactly where the Tunnacliffes' house was, but from the above document it is clear that it stood in that part of Newsome which eventually became known as Tunnacliffe Hill.

The place-name must have been coined between 1570 and 1670, although the evidence is patchy. A rental of 1611, for example, contains a reference to 'Tonyecliffe House' and in 1657 'the occupants of the ground adjacent to Tunycliffe Springe' were told to 'make and repair their fences'. 'Spring' here means a wood and the estate map of 1634 shows these spring woods, close to the house where John Tunicliff was living. One of the most curious versions of the place-name after this was 'Turny Cliffhill Wood' in an estate rental of 1766. In the parish registers of the 1600s the family was still being referred to as 'of Newsome Wood'.[133]

The place-name evidently survived the family's departure from Newsome, for the hearth tax returns include only one Tunnacliffe in 1664 and he was listed under Huddersfield; his name was Isake Tuncliffe and he had been born in Newsome in 1638. There were no Tunnacliffes at all in the returns for 1672 but the parish registers show that Daniel Tunnacliffe was living at Martin Bank later in the century.

In some ways it is tempting to leave the story of Tunnacliffe Hill at this point, but those who know something of the hamlet's later history may be interested in what the Reverend Lewthwaite, vicar of Newsome, wrote over a hundred years ago. He mentions, for example, an important well there which had the reputation of continuing to supply water when other sources had run dry. In the 1880s a stone cover had been built for it, bearing the inscription 'John Jagger and John Sykes, Private Well'. It would be fascinating to know if this was on the spot marked 'John Tunnicliff well' in 1634. Of course, in the Reverend Lewthwaite's day the hamlet had grown considerably in size, and over fifty people were living there. Many of the men were involved in the woollen trade, principally as weavers, but there was a surprising variety of other occupations: George Moore was a blacksmith and farmer, Alf Bottom a mechanic, and Abraham Briggs, a miner. There was also a carter, a moulder and a 'lurryman'. Surprisingly, perhaps, nobody seems to have worked full-time in the nearby quarries operated by Mr Brooke of Fieldhouse.[134]

## Dead Waters, Lockwood

Some years ago there was a long correspondence in the *Huddersfield Examiner* about the Lockwood place-name Dead Waters. Although it is not shown on Ordnance Survey maps it is familiar enough to people in Lockwood, who are accustomed to use it as a 'local' name for St Thomas's road. Various theories were put forward as to how Dead Waters came into use but the most confident explanation came from Peter Walley of Kirkheaton, who wrote that his grandparents had told him how the name had been given to the area after the Holmfirth flood of 1852.

According to them, the debris that was washed down the valley on that day built up in the neighbourhood of Folly Hall and effectively

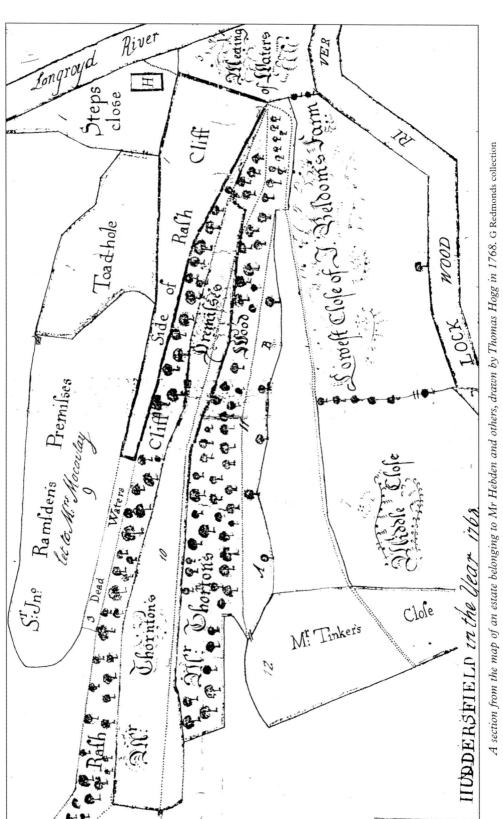

HUDDERSFIELD *in the Year 1768*

*A section from the map of an estate belonging to Mr Hebden and others, drawn by Thomas Hogg in 1768. G Redmonds collection*

*Rashcliffe Hill from Lockwood Road, early 1900s.* Clifford Stephenson

dammed the River Holme close to its junction with the Colne. As a result, the water backed up in the area of Damside, Queen's Mill Road, Albert Street and Folly Hall, forming, eventually, a stagnant lake at the bottom of Rashcliffe Hill. Into this lake were washed the corpses of people and animals drowned in the flood, and they floated there until the authorities dismantled the barrier and secured the bodies for burial.

Ever since, according to this theory, that part of Rashcliffe has always been known as Dead Waters, in memory of the eighty or so victims of the flood. It is a persuasive story but it cannot be true, for we now have evidence that Dead Waters existed as a place-name long before 1852. In fact, it is on the tithe map of Lockwood for 1842 and also on a map of Mr Hebden's estate at Folly Hall of 1768. This shows the area around the confluence of the Holme and the Colne, named as 'Meeting of Waters', and places Dead

Waters right alongside Rash Cliff, a little way from St Thomas's Road.

However, I don't think that we should dismiss Mr Walley's story altogether. The Holmfirth flood was not by any means the first flood in that part of the valley and the circumstances his grandparents described would have been familiar enough in the past. In the diary of Joe William Wilson, a Lockwood tinsmith, there is corroboration of that in an entry for 2 April 1848 – a Sunday. It seems that, after a dreadful storm which lasted for about four hours, the river overflowed into Lockwood's streets, and the people 'coming from church and chapel had to give 1 penny a peece to get over, in cabs and carts'.[135] The local historian H J Morehouse gave an account of several such floods in the Holme Valley, from as far back as 1738, and there must have been many more undocumented.[136] If the water lingered around the 'Meeting of Waters' after such devastation and became stagnant and foul, then Dead Waters would be an apt name, with or without the corpses said to have been there in 1852.

# $\mathscr{D}$ALTON

D alton was a Domesbury vill, no more and no less important than many of its neighbours all those centuries ago, and yet its history has never really been told. That may be explained in part by the fact that it has no nucleus, no village centre; its important houses and hamlets lie scattered right across the township, often linking more readily with neighbouring places than with one another. Greenhead Lane and Bankend, for example, seem to belong to Almondbury rather than to Dalton, and localities along the River Colne have inevitably been drawn into Huddersfield's sphere of influence. Indeed some of them are more usually thought of as part of the town than of Dalton.

## Aspley

Aspley, or 'aspen clearing', appears to have been the former name of land on the Dalton side of the river at Somerset Bridge, although it has come more recently to describe an undefined area around the canal on the Huddersfield side.[137] The low-lying land which rises

*The old canal warehouses at Aspley, 1972. They were demolished in 1974.* Courtesy of the *Huddersfield Examiner*

*Looking north-east from Carr Pit Road, 1964.* Courtesy of the *Huddersfield Examiner*

gently towards Moldgreen was once known as the Storth and although this name is no longer in common use it has survived in Storth Mill, now the home of Shaws' Pickles. The Storth lay in Dalton township and much of it was common grazing or pasture land; its western edge was Penny Dyke which marked the ancient parish boundary between Kirkheaton and Almondbury. The stream is culverted now but its general line is preserved in the shape of Mulberry Street and it can be seen to enter the river just to the east of the bridge. The ancient highway from London to Kendal crossed the River Colne via Huddersfield Bridge but it may not have cut through the Storth as the present Wakefield Road does, and we can only speculate about the exact route in former times. Its importance to local people can be inferred from bequests in early wills. In 1537, for example, William Broke left money towards the mending of Huddersfield Bridge, and he probably lived at Carr Pit, a house on the fringe of the Storth.[138]

It is likely that this was the traditional way between Huddersfield and Almondbury from the earliest phase of Anglian settlement, over 1,300 years ago, and it remained in use into fairly recent times. As tenants of the de Lacys, generations of Huddersfield people would have made their way from Aspley across the Storth and up the bank to Almondbury, en route for the great castle at Pontefract. Eventually, the highway was mapped by Ogilby in 1675 as a section of one of the 'principal roads' in England and, in 1759, local entrepreneurs included it in the turnpike which linked Wakefield and Manchester.

Although 'storth' is a word of Scandinavian origin, signifying, probably, that the land was once covered by brushwood, the first reference to the place-name occurred just over 500 years ago, in the records of Dalton manor court.[139] It is an informative entry for it makes clear that it was then a fenced-in piece of land reclaimed from the waste: to the north was Aspley common and to the south the rough uncultivated terrain of Moldgreen, neither place known to be inhabited at that time. It is also clear that in 1483 it formed part of the estate of Thomas Blackburn, who paid a total rent of four shillings. Curiously, he held one quarter of the Storth as a free-holder and three-quarters as a tenant-at-will.

Although it has not been established just when the Blackburns first came into possession of this valuable piece of land, it was almost certainly much earlier than 1483. The family had figured prominently in Huddersfield records since 1333 at least and their interest in lands in Dalton can be inferred from the number of times they were offenders against the township's by-laws. In 1454, for example, the Dalton constable accused William Blackburn of causing problems for wayfarers because he had not cut his hedges in Aspley Lane, or 'Asppelay loyne' as it was entered in the roll.[140] This suggests that William was already the tenant at Storth, if not in residence there. A number of other entries in the rolls refer to different types of offences: in 1464 Thomas Blackburn 'depastured Dalton Common' with his cattle,[141] whilst an affray that was reported in 1490 involved Richard Blackburn and two Dalton tenants.[142]

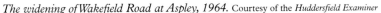

*The widening of Wakefield Road at Aspley, 1964.* Courtesy of the *Huddersfield Examiner*

James Blackburn was apparently the head of this branch of the family from the late 1400s and his name appears in a wide variety of deeds. Prominent amongst these is a Dispensation by the Archbishop of York in 1491, permitting him to marry Lucy Brook, although they were twice related 'within the fourth degree of consanguinity'.[143] James died c.1516 and was succeeded by William. In the subsidy or tax of 1545 William and Thomas Blackburn were listed and it was probably this Thomas who again broke the Dalton bye-laws in 1556, when he illegally enclosed a piece of land near the river.[144]

There is no suggestion in any of these earliest references that the Blackburns lived at Storth. They were usually said to be 'of Huddersfield', and frequently did not take the trouble to attend the Dalton manor court, even though their tenancy of Storth should have made this an obligation. They were, of course, fined for their non-attendance and the money was a steady if very small source of income for the manorial lords of Dalton. The usefulness of these items in the court records is that they help to demonstrate that a house had been built on Storth, possibly at the highway side, and at its southern end close to Moldgreen. For example, in the roll of 1526, William Blackburn's excuses for his absence were offered by 'his tenant William Brook' of Dalton.[145] This, in conjunction with the Dispensation of 1491 and the will of 1537 mentioned earlier, seem to prove that William Brook was living there.

In a variety of early sixteenth century documents, for the period from 1528 to 1576, these Brooks were said to be 'of Carrpitt' in Dalton, which was certainly on the Storth boundary according to later map evidence. However, by the 1560s the Blackburns were ready to relinquish their tenancy and, in doing so, made specific reference to the house. In 1566 John Blackburn of Doncaster, the son of Thomas Blackburn of Huddersfield, released his rights in Storth to William, his elder brother, and clearly referred to 'one messuage or tenement built in the south part of a certain pasture called Storth' and 'two closes of land and meadow abutting on the way leading between Huddersfield and Almondbury'. The document also mentions two other closes 'parcel of the said pasture' and 'a stream called Asplebroke on the west'.[146] This stream was probably the Penny Dyke discussed earlier.

In 1567, the following year, Thomas and William Blackburn sub-let to John Armitage 'a house and two closes' in Dalton and this was probably the same property.[147] Finally, in the court roll of Dalton of 1573 it was recorded that Thomas and William had sold 'the house and lands called Storth' to John Ramsden of Longley; strangely the

*An old name returns. Blackburns take over the former Moldgreen Co-operative stores.* Tony Burke

rent of four shillings was exactly the same as that paid in 1483. Throughout this whole period the occupying sub-tenants were the Brooks.

Certain indirect references to the Storth in these early years are very revealing. For example, in the roll of 1578 it was called an 'essart', a term reserved in the Middle Ages for a woodland clearance that was held by an individual and not the community as a whole. In general, such essarts can be dated to the period 1150-1350 and they had a fence round them, unlike the common fields. No doubt this explains the offences relating to hedgerows mentioned earlier. On another occasion the Storth was referred to as a pasture, part of it seasonally under water, so the inference is that it was a water meadow, deliberately flooded to improve both the soil and the grass. It must have been one of the most valuable pieces of land on the manor and would have been 'enclosed', or sub-divided into smaller fields in the 1500s, a process which gave tenants the chance to introduce changes in husbandry: these are doubtless the 'closes of arable and meadow' referred to in the 1560s.

An event of some local importance occurred in 1581, soon after

*Storths Mill, now Shaw's Pickles, Aspley.* Tony Burke

the Ramsdens took over the tenure of the Storth. At the manor court
Hugh Ramsden was accused of illegally digging for stones 'at the
nether end of mold grene'. At that time the joint owners of Dalton
Manor were John Savile of Wath and Bernard Townley of Hurstwood
in Lancashire, and they chose to make an issue of the offence,
linking it with other minor misdemeanours by the Ramsdens. The
matter came to arbitration, and judgement was announced in an
'award' which chastised John Ramsden for his failure to pay the rent
and for two other offences – not attending the manor court 'for a
tenement called Storth... and for the digging and getting of wall
stones by Hugh Ramsden'. It is possible that these offences had
occurred when the Ramsdens were building their new hall at Lower
Longley *c.*1577. In consequence, John Ramsden was ordered to pay
4s rent, 32s of arrears and furthermore 'to do suit of court'. Mr
Savile and Mr Townley expressed their willingness 'to drop all
actions against Hugh Ramsden' if he agreed to pay these sums
together with 46s 8d costs. The award was made at Over Bradley in
Stainland on 10 October 1582, and the inference is that Ramsden,
as a recent entrant into the ranks of the gentry, was being firmly put
in his place.[148]

## Carr Pit Road

Early Huddersfield maps show that there were, formerly, several meanders in the River Colne downstream from Somerset Bridge, and that much of that riverside land was seasonally under water, probably as part of a deliberate scheme to deposit alluvium on meadows such as the Storth. The names of fields close to the bridge, such as Water Royds and Steanard or Stoneyard confirm this, and Carr Pit is another significant clue to husbandry practices in that part of Huddersfield.

In fact the element 'carr' was generally used of wet areas overgrown with brushwood, very similar in meaning to 'storth', and it was the preferred place-name in those riverside areas where the flooding was controlled. A 'steaner' was a piece of land isolated by a change in the course of the river and 'pits' were regularly found in them: they referred to places where alluvial soil was dug out for use elsewhere in the manor. There are domestic and commercial buildings now where once there were fields called Storth, Water Royd, Steaner and Carr Pit and all that survives today to remind us of that early water management is the place-name Carr Pit Road.

*A section from the map of Huddersfield by George Crosland, 1826.* G Redmonds collection

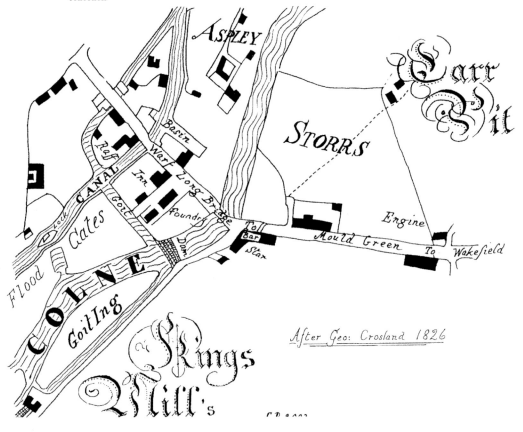

**Dalton deeds – 'life insurance'**

Title deeds are one of the richest sources we have for information about the lives of our ancestors and we shall look at one or two Dalton deeds here to make that point. The first concerns John Appleyard of Dalton and his son George, in 1591, and it highlights the problems that might arise once a father had relinquished control of his property and passed it on to his children. This deed was drawn up to preserve some of the father's rights and, although it might make us smile at times, there is no doubt it dealt with serious issues.

Having diplomatically stressed his affection for his son in the opening part of the deed, John Appleyard then conveyed the family home to him, requesting for himself the right to 'be honestlie and sufficientlie kept and maynteined at the nowe dwellinge howse of the said George... with meat, drink, lodginge and apparell during his natural life'. Clearly nothing could be taken for granted! An unusual request was for George to 'beare the charges of one corslette' or piece of body armour, but we can note in tax rolls of the period that John's assets included such an item. To symbolise the transfer of ownership 'one pewter dishe... and six pence of silver' were to be handed over at the sealing of the documents.

The rightful heir to the estate was actually Richard Appleyard and we are left to speculate why the property was going to George instead. Perhaps he was an invalid, although nothing was said about the matter, apart from the warning that George's entry was not to be prejudicial to Richard. The amusing section of the deed is almost in the nature of an afterthought and as part of it was interlined that may be exactly what it was. It is as though John had wondered if he was being specific enough in asking just for 'meat and drink', and needed reassurance about the quantities involved. To take account of these anxieties George agreed 'to bestow weeklie six pence in ale... and also some pece of rost meate for and towardes the better dietinge of John Appleyearde' for the term of his natural life – except that there was to be no roast meat in Lent. Perhaps, even then, John was not totally reassured – it was after all a time of inflation – so interlined after 'six pence in ale' were the words 'or els three times filling with ale of one flackett which he John Appleyeard brought with him'.[149]

**A deed of partition**

The population started to increase in Elizabeth's reign and one result of that was the need to build more houses which, in turn, resulted in pressure on the commons. Less well known, is the policy of dividing properties or messuages so that two families could be accommodated

*The timber-framed barn at Nether Hall, Dalton.* G Redmonds

and yet scores of deeds preserve the details of such partitions. Typical of these are documents drawn up in 1639 and 1653 between Richard Dyson of Little Carr Green and his son Richard, both yeomen clothiers. The first begins with an itemised list of the lands that belonged to the house and then goes into the details of how the property was divided, calling the father's portion 'the Old Howse' and the son's 'the New Howse'. The building may have been extended in some way but these terms seem certain to refer to the two halves of a single residence.

Along with the Old House the father was to have the dyehouse and an adjoining 'backside', the upper end of the barn, the stable that went with it, and part of the fold. He was also to receive half of each orchard, half the garden and 'one baye of new building'. The difficulties inherent in such partitions are made clear, with each man having half the threshing floor and half of a piece of land in the Lathe Croft, that is the field next to the house where the lathe or barn stood. This was not to be enclosed but 'used in common betwene Richard Dyson thelder and Richard Dyson the yonger; Richard Dyson the yonger to have sufficient wayes, passages, etc. for cartts, carriages... over and through the saide back fold'.

The second half of the agreement dealt with the son's portion and naturally some of the shared items were those just referred to. There was, though, an interesting description of the 'New House' which included 'all the howsinge from the old pann of the old howse eastwards, the nether baye of the barne, the mistall thereunto adioyninge, the swinecoate' and a number of named closes. There was a right of way for carts, carriages and 'drifte of cattle' through a field called Greatstandlawe, but this was restricted when corn had been sown, at which time both parties were required to fetch and drive their cattle over the common.

Fourteen years later, when no fewer than five men had interests in Lathe Croft, it was felt that the agreement regarding this close needed to be made much clearer, principally because Richard Dyson the younger wished to place his tenter frame there. Several interesting clauses dealt with this and associated problems, and a piece of land was set aside in the upper end of the croft, described as 'one tenterrowme', in which he might 'fix and sett one tenter... with sufficient wayes and passage to and from the same'. These had to include 'wayes... for John Northe... for the carryinge of hay and corne in the harveste time to the barn dore.' The agreement about the water alerts us to customary practices in husbandry locally and it is worth quoting in the original words:

> *The sayd partyes shall for ever have the benifitt of the water course and the current thereof runninge into the close called Lathe, with liberty to turne the same into his and theire rateable parte...to his and their most profit...and liberty to clense the watercourse soe often as neede shall requier in such sorte as hath bene formerly used and accustomed...and also liberty to clense the pond belonginge the messuage by turne for ever yearly. And he or they who shall soe clense the same to have the benefitt of the clensing to their owne uses.*[150]

## Moldgreen

In Dalton there were, in earlier centuries, several uncultivated pieces of land where all the tenants had grazing rights for their animals, as

*Almondbury Bank from Moldgreen. The Methodist chapel was demolished after a serious fire.* Clifford Stephenson

in other townships locally. Such areas were described in manorial documents as the wastes and commons, and one clue to their location is the word 'green', in place-names such as Carr Green, Greenside and Moldgreen. The court rolls for Dalton confirm that Moldgreen was indeed 'waste' in this sense, and several tenants incurred penalties for unlawfully enclosing land there. In 1526 one guilty party was Richard Cowper of Dalton – although the ground he had appropriated was only 'the sixth part of a rood'. In 1559 Thomas Atkinson enclosed a rather bigger piece, for which he was made to pay twelve pence fine. There are entries in the court rolls for a variety of offences which emphasise this aspect of the locality's history.

As we have seen, Hugh Ramsden was fined for illegally digging stones from the lower end of Moldgreen in 1581 while, in 1655, Miriam Armitage was fined 3s 4d 'for having brought geese to feed upon Mold Green', contrary to the bye-laws of the manor.[151] There is nothing in these references to indicate when the first dwelling was built at Moldgreen, but entries for the Hirst family suggest that it was early in the reign of Henry VIII. In 1515 the surname Hirst appeared in the list of Dalton tenants for the first time and, in a tithe rental of 1558, Roger Hirst was said to be 'of Mold Green'.[152] The surname has been recorded there at regular intervals ever since, which may imply that the Hirsts are Moldgreen's longest established family.

Almost a century may have passed before the Hirsts were joined at Moldgreen by other tenants, but the evidence suggests that by 1700 it was a well-established community of possibly half a dozen families. The names recorded there in this period all had local origins, but not one of them had its origins in the township, i.e. Brook, Hirst, Firth, Spivey, Blackburn and Greenwood.

A more important aspect of the locality's early history concerns its position at the junction of important highways. The ancient route from Huddersfield to the south reached Moldgreen via Somerset Bridge but the traveller then had a choice of routes; the London road headed in a south-easterly direction up Almondbury Bank, while the local highway went forward by way of Broad Lane and Carr Green Lane. This route had been mentioned in the court rolls of 1486[153] and was called 'lytill carr layne' in 1519. As late as 1719 it was described as the King's highway between Huddersfield and 'Leeheadbridge'.[154]

From the Quarter Sessions Order Book of 1733 we learn that the traveller, who was faced with such a choice of routes, would find 'a stone or post' at the crossroads 'with an inscription thereon in Large Letters containing the name of the next Markett Town'. However, before the erection of such guide stoops the junction was marked by a stone pillar or cross, and there is no doubt that such a cross stood at one time at the foot of Almondbury Bank. It is referred to in

*The* Waterloo Hotel, *named after the bridge was built in 1819.* G Redmonds collection

Warburton's survey of the road in 1720 and the approximate site is commemorated in the public house known as *Green Cross*.

The locality changed decisively in the nineteenth century. The new Turnpike Road to Wakefield, via Waterloo Bridge, was built *c*.1820 and then, in 1850, the Lister Kaye family put their Moldgreen land up for sale, a decision which made possible the speculative building that established the Victorian character of the suburb. Perhaps the only reminders of early Moldgreen, apart from the name of the *Green Cross Inn*, are a few old cottages at the heart of the community.

**The Green Cross**

George Batley was the licensee of the *Green Cross Inn* in the late 1850s and he kept an account book which was passed down to his descendants. It provides a fascinating insight into the life of a publican some 140 years ago.

It was perhaps inevitable in a working class community that the local innkeeper should extend credit to his customers and one part of the accounts records such debts, mostly for modest sums of two or three shillings. Occasionally, however, the agreements were more formally entered into the book in a more legal style. For example in May 1862 George Batley advanced £5 to James Spivey, the latter agreeing 'to pay ten per cent per annum for the same'. This loan was extended by a further £1 in December. It seems also that the innkeeper was prepared to barter, for in 1863 he noted the receipt of 35s from Aeneas Watson 'making a balance of rent with potatoes, etc.'. Later, he recorded the receipt of a 'horse and cart in exchange for 26 thousand bricks'.

It is amusing to see that certain customers merited a 'Mr' before their name, suggesting that in the publican's opinion they were gentry. This applied to Mr Atkinson, the local mill owner, and also to a Mr Pearson who had expensive tastes and owed money for whisky, brandy, rum and gin. More often the entries related to individuals referred to more familiarly as Johney Schorfield, Billy Popelton or Andy Tailor – even just Fish Joe on one occasion. On those occasions the purchases were usually 'ale and bacco' or even 'ale and setra'. A popular drink of the period was ginger beer or, as George Batley called it, 'Gingerite'. The recipe for this was written on a separate page and in a much more elegant hand and it included 'tincture of capsicums' and 'a little tartarice to tast'.

A number of entries appear to have had little to do with the innkeeping business. They record sums of 18s and 16s from Mr Atkinson for new boots and there are other entries for shoes soling and heeling.

*The* Green Cross *at Moldgreen. It was so named originally because there was a cross at the road junction.* Tony Burke

Perhaps George Batley had been a shoemaker by trade before taking over the *Green Cross* and was prepared to supplement his income by accepting a few commissions, or perhaps he acted as an agent for local tradesmen. He actually described himself as 'agent and gamester' but this title probably referred to his activities as a bookmaker.

Numerous bets are entered into the accounts and there are references to the Derby, the Cambridgeshire and the Chester Cup. When the last of these was run, in 1861, George Batley organised a sweep in which thirteen of his neighbours took part. They paid 1s each, of which the winner took 10s and the second 2s; the third recovered his stake. On another occasion William Bradley 'bett George Batley £7 to £1 that Lord Clifton dont win the St Leger'; he also bet three to one that the horse would not be placed. The names of these long-dead runners were just as picturesque as those of today: Millionaire, Umpire, Man at Arms, Chere Amie and Flirtation.

George Batley was certainly literate and he made his own entries in the book, but the writing is variable, the spelling erratic and occasionally dialect creeps in. We can easily identify Tuncliff, Horst and Logwood as the names of men called Tunnacliffe, Hirst and Lockwood, but 'poshen' for possession is more difficult. The word 'launce' must surely be for 'lowance', that is an allowance or credit, a term still in occasional use.

The innkeeper may have died *c.*1870, for after that the handwriting changes and Sarah Ann Batley seems to be in charge. From the later entries, and a few papers surviving with the accounts, it is clear that the family's property consisted of more than just a public house. There were a few cottages, several shops (a saddler's is mentioned and a butcher's) and they also rented out stables, sheds, 'a long room over the warehouse', and space in the yard for Moldgreen local board to keep its equipment. One way and another the money came in and by 1878 Sarah Ann Batley was able to make a payment in excess of £500 to clear the mortgage and interest.

## Ravensknowle

In one sense there are three major phases in the history of Ravensknowle. The best documented is undoubtedly the period since 1827 when the old property there was sold by auction and made way for the villa and grounds that are today's Tolson Museum. Nothing remains of that older house, which was lived in by a branch of the Hirst family for generations, but the history of its owners is well documented: the landlords included the Dightons (who took their

*The side entrance to Ravensknowle Park. The stone gateway is from the old Cloth Hall.* G Redmonds

name from Deighton), the Wheatleys, the Knights of the Hospital of St John and the Lister Kayes. That earlier building, on a different site from the present villa, is recorded from the 1400s and may go back even earlier, but the fact remains that the place-name referred originally to the prominent hill behind the house and not to the house itself. It means the 'raven's knoll', and was clearly identified and named in the earliest surviving boundary perambulation of Almondbury.

### Rawthorpe Hall

Rawthorpe Hall is a fine old house and a rare survival in the Huddersfield area, its great antiquity masked by the casing of stone, slate and brick, materials which reflect its chequered history. The stonework of the façade dates from different periods but the windows in particular indicate that much of it is of relatively recent date, whilst the elegant hand-made bricks in the wall of the east wing may have been put there in the eighteenth century. The doorways, both front and rear, date from the seventeenth century and confirm the existence of an earlier hearth passage, and there is a three-light stone-mullioned window in the east wing from the same period.

At first glance, this patchwork exterior offers no clue to the timber-framed house at the core of the building – a house judged to have

*Rawthorpe Hall, Dalton, a typical gentry house of the early sixteenth century, with an open hall and cross wings, 1995.* Courtesy of the *Huddersfield Examiner*

*A blocked-in doorway on the front face of Rawthorpe Hall, 1995.* Courtesy of the *Huddersfield Examiner*

been built almost five hundred years ago. Nevertheless, the plan of the hall, with its central house-body and cross wings is characteristic of the late medieval period, and the position of the hearth passage and chimney indicate that the central bays were open to the roof. Access to the chambers in the west wing was probably via a stairway built into a lean-to on the front face, while the pattern of stone-work on the south gable of the east wing clearly suggests an original jettied upper storey.

Strangely, even in its present much-altered state, the house tells us more about early Rawthorpe than do any surviving records, for that period in Dalton's history is not well documented. The suffix 'thorpe' certainly suggests that an early settlement existed on the site but the place-name has not been recorded before 1473, when it formed part of the compound 'Rawthorployne'.[155] For evidence of a family living there we have to wait until the 1500s, when the Langleys or Longleys owned the property. It was claimed by some that this family had links with Thomas Langley, who was the Bishop of Durham (1406-27) and served as Lord Chancellor to both Henry IV and Henry V, and a pedigree in Dugdale's Visitation of 1665 purports to illustrate that connection. Legh Tolson, the Kirkheaton historian,[156] also suggested that they were originally a branch of the Lancashire Langleys, but both these claims should be treated with great caution, for the evidence shows that there were Langleys of modest status living in Dalton from the 1370s at least. It is quite possible, therefore, that the surname derives from Longley in Almondbury.

The court rolls show that various members of this family held the office of constable for Dalton through the 1400s, and Henry Langley was a free tenant of the manor from *c.*1480. Richard Langley was living at Rawthorpe when he died prematurely in September 1537 and it is likely that he was the builder of the original timber-framed hall. He was certainly the first member of the family to be described in deeds as a 'gentleman', and the same title was regularly accorded to two of his sons. It is interesting, therefore, to speculate on what part the Beaumonts played in this raised status, for Richard's wife was Joan, or Jane, Beaumont of Lascelles Hall, and her father Thomas had earlier married Agnes Langley.

Legh Tolson recorded another interesting chapter in the history of the Langleys, when he described how one branch moved away from Huddersfield, like so many other local gentry families. Richard Langley married Agnes Hansby of New Malton and they established themselves at Grimthorpe in the Pocklington area. He was a staunch Catholic and when he refused to abandon his beliefs, after the break with Rome, he found himself accused of hiding visiting papist priests and others of the old religion. When he was tried and hanged at York in 1586, a martyr to that faith, there was certainly reference to priest holes and sympathies with Rome.

The Rawthorpe property had, meanwhile, passed to his brother Arthur, and the last of the family to possess Rawthorpe Hall was John who is said to have died in 1717, by which time a family called Walker was living in the house. From about the same period there were also Walkers at Lascelles Hall close by, who are likely to have been kinsmen, and both houses seem to have entered a period of decline. The house finally passed into the possession of Huddersfield Corporation in 1919, having belonged at different times to the Lister Kayes and the Ramsdens. When he recorded the demolition of part of the property and the conversion of the remainder into cottages, Tolson noted that a dilapidated plaster coat of arms of the Langleys was, unfortunately, destroyed at the same time.

# $\mathcal{L}$INDLEY AND FIXBY

N ow, when the townships of the ancient parish of Huddersfield are discussed, Lindley is usually linked with Quarmby, and it is Lindley that is seen as the more important of the two. In 1086 both were independent estates, but that must have changed quite soon afterwards, for there are several fourteenth century charters and deeds which describe Lindley at that time as lying within Quarmby.[157] That relationship had not changed by the sixteenth century when Lindley was still said to be a hamlet of Quarmby, nor by 1627 when John Clay died, for he was described as a yeoman 'of Nether Linley in Quernebye'.[158]

In fact the size and status of Quarmby have changed so much in recent years that its former importance is all but forgotten, and it is thought of as a fairly limited territory, stretching from Haughs in the west to Reinwood Road in the east. To the north would probably be New Hey Road, but the southern limit would be much less easy to define, probably stopping short of Longwood Road. Right at the heart of the area would be Quarmby Fold, huddled round its ancient hall. In any event, the area would be seen now as part of Huddersfield and, in terms of size and population, not a very significant one.

As we have seen, though, it was Quarmby that had township status in earlier centuries, not Lindley, and within its boundaries there were other places that have usually been thought of as having independent histories. Its full extent is explicit in the hearth tax of 1672, when the return for Quarmby included the 'quarters' of Lindley, Golcar, Longwood, Scammonden and North Crosland. That same status is made clear in a wide variety of early documents. Localities such as Mole's Head, Outlane and Slack, all part of Longwood, were often described in the past as being in Quarmby – Mole's Head as late as 1633. Even Golcar itself, mentioned in Domesday Book, was said in the reign of Henry VII to be in Quarmby, and a deed in 1512 mentions 'lands in Wharmeby called Crymble' quitclaimed to Richard Beaumont of Whitley Hall.[159] That pushes the township's boundary to the south-west as far as Crimble Clough and Slaithwaite, whilst to the north-west it was on Pole Moor where, in 1761, there was 'a certain bounder stone... called Slaighthwaite Poll dividing the townships of Slaithwaite and Quarmby'.[160] The Scammonden hamlet of Croft House near Pole Moor was certainly in Quarmby according to the will of Margaret Bottomley, in 1599,

*West Street, Lindley, c.1900. The* Red Lion *was on the left and the premises of Earnshaw Brothers on the right, but all these buildings have been demolished.* G Redmonds collection

*Quarmby Hall in the early 1900s.* Clifford Stephenson

and a deed of 1615 places even Deanhead in the same township.

Perhaps the most interesting information in this respect relates to localities which have always been in Linthwaite and Lockwood, making it clear that the Colne was not the southern boundary for Quarmby. This is apparent in a reference in the Sessions Rolls of 1597, referred to earlier, which described Longroydbridge as 'standing betwene the Towneships of Huddersfeild and Quarmebie'. Indeed, in 1677 North Crosland was referred to as lying 'in the constablerie of Quarmby' and, at different times, the hamlets of Cowlersley (1497), Wiggin Cross (1591) and Flat House (1676) were all said to be in the township. All these were of course in Almondbury parish.

The first document which suggests that this vast township was becoming too unwieldy to administer is the Protestation Return of 1642, in which Scammonden, Lindley, Longwood and Golcar appeared under separate headings for the first time. It was a temporary status, as the later hearth tax returns prove, but pressure for change was coming from Quarmby itself and, in 1648, there was an appeal to the authorities by the overworked constable. It brought the following reply:

> *The Courte, takeinge into consideracion the vastness of the Constablerie, conceive that the service of the kingdome cannot by him bee performed without good assistance and therefore thinks fitting that*

*the several hamletts yeild him assistance in his office, affording him a deputy or other assistant, else the Courte will be forced presently to charge each hamlett to fynde a constable of themselves.*[161]

Unfortunately, it is not yet clear exactly when the final break-up took place, but it cannot have been before 1761 when Pole Moor was still the boundary. However, some of the hamlets appear to have won independence by 1822, when the township name was Quarmby-with-Lindley.[162] The boundary between these two 'hamlets' was being discussed at a public meeting in Lindley School that same year,[163] but the argument may still have been unresolved in the 1840s, when the first Ordnance Survey maps describe localities such as Birchencliffe and Warren House as 'Quarmby detached'. However, OS maps drawn within the last few decades provide conclusive evidence of Quarmby's decline, confining the name to the few houses around the still impressive Quarmby Hall. One of the few reminders now of the

*Prince Royd, Birchencliffe, in the early 1900s.* Clifford Stephenson

great days is the allegiance to Longwood of the scattered farms of Haigh House Hill, a thin, triangular territory lying on the Elland side of the watershed with Halifax ancient parish.

### Lindley open field enclosure

There is an important map of Lindley in the Thornhill papers. Although it is undated, it seems certain to relate to a 1799 survey of 'Severall Parcells of Land divided from... Lindley Fields to Thomas Thornhill, Esq.'.[164] Its purpose was to show those parts of the town fields where enclosure had taken place by private agreement and the tenants were 'to subdivide the in fences at their own expences'. However, the map almost incidentally throws considerable light on pre-enclosure Lindley, confirming what place-names had only hinted at – that the original axis of the village was east to west. That line of road is now appropriately East Street and West Street. To the south lay the open fields, still in strips, and accessible no doubt via the 'Lidgate' or swing gate. The whole development of the village along today's Lidget Street, past Field House and Acre Mills, is therefore relatively new, and all three place-names are a reminder of the medieval field system.

By the 1790s these strips were in the tenancy of a few men only and this may have hastened their enclosure. The principal owner was Thomas Thornhill, but five other men, William Heaton, William Waterhouse, Thomas Oldfield, James Wilkinson and Thomas Firth, all held strips running parallel to the Lidgate Lane, or Lidget Street. Some enclosure had already taken place in the fields towards where the Clock Tower now stands and owners represented there were John Lindley, John Thwaite, Joseph Radcliffe, Esq., and Thomas Thornton's trustees.

There were, of course, no mills, no chapels and no church – just a few scattered cottages along the strip of waste at the north end of the fields. Furthermore, there was no Halifax Road through Birchencliffe and no New Hey Road. In fact, much of the value of the map lies in the information it provides about the history of today's roads and paths. What we call Plover Road, for example, was then Sparth Lane, a direct link between the village and the hamlet of Oakes, now isolated by the New Hey Road. Sparth was an old word meaning 'sheep-droppings' and even in the 1700s it was being confused with 'spark', which is how the name survives in Sparks Road, a fragment of a lane to the south of New Hey Road. At that time Plover was simply the name of one of the adjoining fields.

The area between this road and Crosland Road, much of it now

*The Clock Tower in Lindley, photographed from the churchyard. It was built in 1902 and Edgar Wood was the architect. It stands where five roads converge.* Tony Burke

built over, belonged entirely to Mr Thornhill, and part of it was called Law Hill. This was the site of an important well, linked to the open fields by a 'sough' or water channel . The word 'law' meant hill and could go back to the earliest years of Lindley's settlement. It is ironic that as 'law' became obsolete the not very prominent mound became first Law Hill and finally the present Low Hill.

The period of the Parliamentary Enclosures saw the creation of many new roads, some of which were newly-built 'occupation' roads. They were often straight and I had always assumed that Lindley's Occupation Road dated from the time of the enclosure, but the map shows quite clearly that it came into existence during the earlier open field enclosure and had the status of a footpath. It was called Springs Road and dropped down to a small stream at the 'Beggars Stile', roughly where Sunny Bank Road now runs into Cleveland Road. The place-name Sunny Bank is on record from 1775 and may be much older. Where the Clock Tower stands was, even then, the point where five routes converged and today's Daisy Lea Lane was the direct footpath to Birkby. Something of its past is still evoked by the narrow and secretive 'snicket' which continues into Birkby beyond Halifax Road.

Finally, the map has solved at least one long-standing problem.

*Sparks Road, Oakes, formerly 'Sparth'.* Tony Burke

*A 'snicket' off Halifax Road; the eastern end of the old footway from Lindley to Birkby.* Tony Burke

Long before the turnpike era, an unidentified part of the highway from Huddersfield to Lindley was called Hole or Hoyle Lane, a name which seems not to have survived. However, the map shows that in the 1790s a lane ran from where the *Bay Horse* now stands to the top of Luck Lane; at the Lindley end the words Hole Lane Gate suggest that this was one end of the 'lost' Hoyle Lane. The name probably died out once the land had been incorporated into the new turnpike, *c.*1806.

## Salendine Nook

The settlement at Salendine Nook is well over 450 years old and much of its later history is tied up with the Morton family and the Baptist Chapel. Percy Stocks wrote about that connection in *Foundations* (1933), but he found no separate reference to the Nook

*The* Spotted Cow *at Salendine Nook, early 1900s. Courtesy of the* Huddersfield Examiner

SPOTTED COW INN
"TOM WOOD"

INE NOOK LINDLEY

before 1707 and assumed that the name came into being about that period. However, it is mentioned quite frequently in the sixteenth and seventeenth centuries and was noted by Crump as early as 1533, when 'William Hague late of Salnden' was one of numerous Huddersfield clothiers who were said to have deceitfully made woollen cloth 'with woofe called flocks'.[165] This spelling of the name may indicate how it was pronounced at that time.

There is now additional evidence which implies that for most of the sixteenth century Salendine Nook, or Salendine as it was also called, was the name of a single house occupied by a branch of the Haigh family. The actual tenants, at least in the 1560s, were probably the Ramsdens of Longley, as freeholders in the manor of Quarmby, for a rental in one of their account books includes 'William Haghe of Salenden' (1561). He may have been the son of Crump's clothier. A rental eight years later in the same accounts contains the name John Haghe of Salenden, which suggests that William had died. In fact there is a burial entry in Huddersfield parish register in 1569 for a Haigh of 'Salanden noke', but the christian name is not clear.

At that time Salendine Nook was in the manor of Quarmby, jointly held by the Eltofts and the Blythes, and in 1572 Edmond Eltoftes of Rysheworthe Hall near Bingley leased half of his moiety of 'a messuage called Salondynenoke' to 'Edwards Haghe of Salandynenoke'. He was the son of Henry Haghe of Longwood, a husbandman not a clothier, and Edward was to hold the property for a term of twenty-one years, at a rent of 11s 6d.[166] Perhaps the house was already being sub-divided to accommodate more than one family. Unfortunately, this old homestead has long since disappeared and even its site is not certain. One possibility is that it was on land which became part of the chapel graveyard, for it was there, according to Percy Stock, that a block of farm buildings once stood.

This seems more likely when we consider that the first chapel was built on land owned by the Mortons, who were then said to be of Salendine Nook. Much has been written about the arrival of this family in Lindley and they were famous potters in their day. However, most of the accounts are quite inaccurate, as Percy Stock was able to show, and all we know for certain is that a Janet Morton was living at Salendine Nook in the1590s. The important rental of Quarmby for 1609 links the names of Edward Haigh and Widow Morton 'for Sallindine nowke' at a rent of 1s ½d, so it would not be surprising if Widow Morton were in fact Janet Morton, nee Haigh.[167] Incidentally, the rent paid in 1609 was exactly the same as that paid by John Haigh in 1569. Sadly, there is nothing to suggest that the Mortons were potters at that time although several books claim that they were. The earliest evidence for pot-making is not until the mid-1700s and the tradition came to an end a few years ago when Harold Morton died.

## Fixby

No account of Huddersfield and its environs can afford to ignore Fixby, although in the past it was actually an outlying part of Halifax parish. Now it is more often thought of as a suburb of Huddersfield, partly because there has been a good deal of building there in recent times, much of it in the southern half of the township. However, there are historical reasons also behind the shift in 'allegiance', notably the confusion surrounding the boundary between the two. The rivulet which runs through the Grimescar valley is the one which further downstream was formerly called the 'Town Brook' and divides Huddersfield from Fartown; in its upper reaches it appears to be the natural boundary between Huddersfield and Halifax. However, the locations of the major springs and feeder streams in that area gave rise to arguments about which township the land on its banks belonged to, and these persisted into the 1800s.

*A view from Fixby looking towards the Calder Valley.* G Redmonds collection

*Fixby Hall, 1986.* Courtesy of the *Huddersfield Examiner*

### A Scandinavian place-name

Fixby is an intriguing place-name, for one of its two Scandinavian elements is very distinctive. That is not the case with the suffix 'by', which means a settlement and is familiar to us both locally and right across the county, but the first element is said by Scandinavian experts to derive from an Old Irish personal name 'Fiacc', and that is unusual, for it would mean that the settlement was created by Norwegian Vikings rather than Danes. These Norsemen arrived from the west, not from the east, having invaded Cumbria and North Lancashire from Ireland, where they had been settled for several generations. From there they moved across the Pennines into west Yorkshire, and Fixby is one of several place-names, in and around the Colne Valley, with a possible Norwegian derivation. Two others are Golcar and Crosland, located in an area where Scandinavian names abound, e.g. Quarmby, Sowerby, Slaithwaite, Linthwaite, Holme[168] and Lingards.

These Norsemen were herdsmen, not farmers, and their settlements tended to be on the higher land, in scattered farmhouses rather than nucleated villages, which might mean that Fixby was never much more than a few dispersed dwellings.[169] In fact, it had no known centre right into modern times, although the assumption has been that it once had a nucleus and was then depopulated, possibly when the land was originally emparked. For that reason Fixby Hall has sometimes been thought of as lying on the site of the original village. The place-name 'Old Towne Yerdes' features in a document of 1445 and it has been suggested that this refers to such a former settlement.[170]

In the post-Conquest period Fixby became part of Halifax parish, and it was then linked with a number of other townships to form the chapelry of Elland. Its manorial ties were with Wakefield manor but that status was complicated by the fact that its northern half remained in the graveship of Rastrick, in demesne, whilst the southern half became a sub-manor and was held from the twelfth century by a succession of landlords. Among these were the Beaumonts, for a short time, and the Thornhills.

## Lightridge

When the residents of Fixby were taxed in 1379, the total population of the township must have been very small indeed, since one name only appeared on the list of residents, that of Lightridge. It may be that some families who actually lived there were not recorded for some reason, but even so it is a remarkable statististic. Those taxed were William de Lythering, his wife, and two daughters, Annabilla and Magota. William's ancestors had been prominent in the district from the beginning of the century and I have seen it said that they were a younger branch of the 'de Fekesbys'. That may be true and it has been suggested that Richard de Lythriche, who released land to James de Eland in 1324, was in fact the son of Thomas de Fekesby. However, the truth is that the surname Lightridge is found in the court rolls of Wakefield manor some time before that. In 1307, for

*Lightridge House, on or close to the site of a medieval settlement.* Tony Burke

example, Thomas de Lytherigge paid twelve pence to the court for licence to take half an acre from the lord's waste in Fixby and just one year later Robert de Lythrige and Thomas de Totehill were involved in a plea of debt.[171] After that there are scores of references to successive generations of the family, right through the 1300s, but the last example I have noted is in 1402 when Adam del Lyghtherig, the son of William, granted his lands in Fixby to Thomas de Dalton.[172] He may have been the last to bear the surname.

It is the surname of course which provides much of the early evidence for the place-name but fortunately there are several independent references to Lightridge in early title deeds, and they describe it either as a territory or as a 'messuage'. In the late thirteenth century, for example, 'Thomas de Fixby enfeoffed John del Wood of a piece of land lying between Bradley Wood and 'Robberode of Lyteriche, the whole to be held of the lord of the fee for the annual rent of 2 shillings'. Other men named in the deed were Thomas de Toothill and Richard de Ainley, and all those mentioned bore surnames with local origins, helping to confirm that Lightridge lay on the hilly spur which separates Huddersfield from the Calder Valley.[173] By the end of the thirteenth century this part of Fixby had passed from the Beaumonts to Thomas de Toothill, probably the man mentioned in the above deed and when his granddaughter married Richard de Thornhill, her second husband, the possession of Lightridge passed into the hands of a family who held it, in an unbroken line of descent, into the middle of the nineteenth century.

We cannot be certain how extensive Lightridge was, nor even precisely where it lay, although it must have been close to where Lightridge House now stands. We might expect it to feature regularly in Elland parish registers but for some reason it is scarcely mentioned in the early volumes. Fortunately, it occurs often enough in other sources to provide us with an outline of its history in the fifteenth and sixteenth centuries and, from the late 1500s, we have the names of the tenants, including Wilkinson and Brook. Edward Brooke is referred to on a number of occasions: first, in 1658, when it was reported at the manor court that he 'did digge upon the soile and gett stones near the highway upon Reape Hirst'[174] and then again in 1676 when he paid rent of 3s 4d 'for Letridg'. A poignant entry in the diary of Oliver Heywood tells us that in 1679 'Joshua Brooke of Litteridg in Fixby, that marryed Richard Appleyard's daughter, going drunk from Halifax...was found dead in the way home with one foot in the stirrup, his horse standing over him.'[175] His wife was pregnant with their fourth child. In 1709, according to Wakefield manorial records,

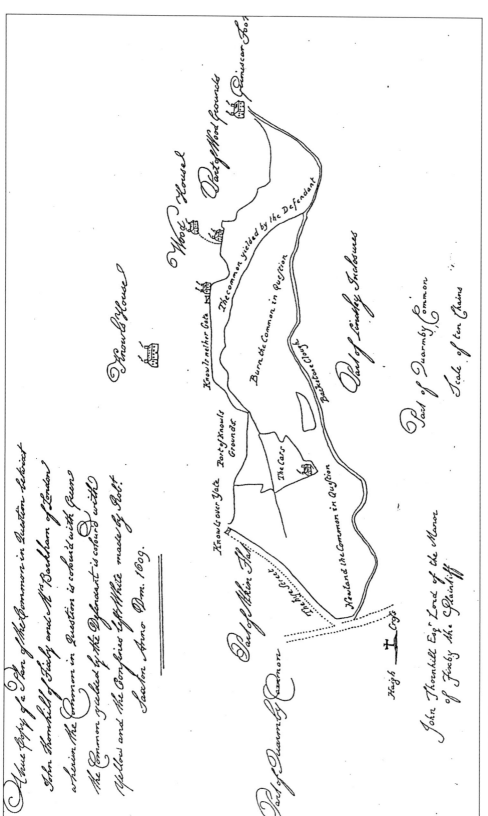

A true Copy of a Plott of the Common in Question betwixt
John Thornhill of Fixby and Mr Backham of London?
wherein the Common in Question is coloured with Greene
the Common yielded by the Defendant is coloured with
Yellow and the Confines left White made by Robt.
Saxton Anno Dm. 1609.

Part of Astler Hall

The high street

Haigh Cote

Part of Quarmby Common

Part of Quarmby Common

Knowls over Yate

Newland the Common in Question

Part of Knowls Grounds

The Cars

The Common in Question

Knowls nether Gate

The Common yielded by the Defendant

Burn the Common in Question

Brickstone Clough

Knowls House

Knowls House

Wool Housel

Part of Wood Grounds

Grimescar Foot

Part of Lindley Inclosures

Part of Quarmby Common

Scale of ten Chains

John Thornhill Esqr Lord of the Manor
of Fixby the Plaintiff

*Robert Saxton's map of the Grimescar Valley 1609, from a copy made during a much later dispute. G Redmonds collection* a man called Emmanuel Roulston was the tenant of the farm called 'Lighteredge' owned by Thomas Thornhill.[176]

The meaning of a place-name can often throw some light on its location, but in the case of Lightridge the modern spelling is deceptive. It is tempting to think of the early settlement lying on the ridge in a south-facing direction but in fact the earliest forms of the word prove that the suffix was not 'ridge' but the Old English word 'ric', found also in Rastrick. This word was sometimes used for a narrow track, so it may be that Lightridge was originally nearer the line of the old highway which lead from Cowcliffe to Elland Upper Edge – or even the ancient right-of-way across Fixby Park. The truth is that a number of routes of varying importance climbed this hillside, linking Bradley and Huddersfield with Elland, so Lightridge could have been connected with any one of them.

## The Wood

If we try to imagine our local landscape as it was when the first Anglian settlers knew it, over 1,300 years ago, we must picture their settlements as small groups of dwellings, separated from the encircling trees by a few crofts and patches of cultivated land. From most hill tops there would have been an almost unbroken vista of forest stretching away to the horizon, with only a plume of smoke here and there to tell us where the hamlets were. The word the settlers used for each tiny cleared area was 'ley' and it is commemorated in numerous place-names; Farnley, for example, Honley, Shelley, Lindley and many, many more. The encircling trees were the 'wood', for it was the French-speaking Normans who introduced the word forest. As the population increased there were hungry mouths to feed and more land was brought under the plough, extending the cultivated area and eating away at the woodland. When the original hamlets eventually became too crowded new settlements had to be established in the wood.

It is a story of exploitation and colonisation common to most of our local townships, and it explains why certain fields along Lucy Lane in Lepton are still called Old Wood Closes, and why the place-name Woodhouse, meaning literally the 'house in the wood', occurs over and over again locally. Emley, Shelley, Rastrick and Huddersfield, for example, all have their Woodhouse, originally a single dwelling some distance from the main settlement. Occasionally, more than one house was built; Woodsome in Farnley Tyas derives from the dative plural of 'Woodhouse' and meant 'at the houses in the wood'. And there are other common place-names such

*The Wood, Fixby, 1995. Today's handsome house is on the site of a medieval settlement.* Courtesy of the *Huddersfield Examiner*

as Woodhead, Woodbottom, or even just Wood itself, which all tell the same story. Most of these settlement names are at least 400 years old and one of the latest I have been able to identify is the house in Farnley Tyas known as the Wood; it dates from Elizabeth's reign, by which time only a small percentage of that early forest remained.

Most of the hamlets are very much older and we can only speculate about their origins but there is a house in Fixby known as the Wood which looks out across the Grimescar Valley towards Birchencliffe and Lindley and is well enough documented for us to put together something of its history. In 1609 the upper part of the valley was at the centre of a dispute between John Thornhill of Fixby Hall and Mistress Barkham. This lady lived in London but held the lordship of Quarmby and the argument concerned the stream in the valley bottom which was the boundary between their respective estates. The problem was that the stream had two important feeders which flowed down from Lindley Moor to the south-west and it was the ownership of the land in the triangle thus formed that was being debated. This included Burn Common, and new land close to what is now the Warren House. The matter had arisen because the Wood and its land had just come into the Thornhills' possession, conveyed to them by Edward Saltonstall, but previously 'the inheritance of Agnes, daughter and heiress of John Wood, late of the Wood'.[177]

It is this last item of information which is intriguing. Title deeds once in the Thornhills' keeping, reveal that an important family called Wood had lived in the township from the thirteenth century. The inference is that they derived their surname from the settlement in Grimescar Wood and remained there as tenants into the late 1500s. An even earlier deed, of *c.*1200, actually refers to a thirteen-acre clearing in the wood which may predate the house. Today's landscape therefore, takes us back possibly 800 years, to the time when this part of Grimescar Wood was cleared and the land was brought under cultivation. The woodland still forms the boundary to the south-east, and plantations on the northern ridge that are part of Fixby Hall estate help to recreate the earlier landscape. From across the valley, even the eighteenth century turnpike to Halifax is masked from our view by stone walls and does not intrude on the imagination. To the west lies Knowles, a place with an even older name.

**Knowles**

The cluster of buildings at Knowles has a much longer history than we might think, for the place-name is found as 'Knauewellehirst' in a land grant of *c.*1200.[178] The first part of this is interpreted as 'the youths' well' and it occurs in several related place-names in the same part of Fixby. These make it clear that the name had nothing to do with 'knoll' in the sense of a rounded hill, even though later spellings show that it was influenced by that word. The inference from early compounds such as 'Knawelker' (1286) and 'Knawalrodhenge' (1358) is that 'Knowles' was originally the name of an extensive territory. The 'ker' or marsh was probably close to Carrs farm, just to the east of Warren House, and the 'rod' was an essart or 'royd' which we cannot now identify. In another grant, dated 1358, a piece of land was said to lie between this essart and 'Adecok Neweland', possibly the earlier form of Adkin or Acton Flatt.[179]

There is nothing in these early charters to tell us whether the settlement at Knowles dates from the same period. An isolated reference in the court rolls mentions an Ainley tenant unlawfully putting up a hedge in 'Knolles' in 1437 and John Chaloner of Ainley 'unjustly made a way for all manner of carts' there in 1458, all which tends to suggest that Ainley and Knowles shared a common

*Knowles in Fixby, a place-name that goes back to the thirteenth century at least.*
Tony Burke

boundary.[180] However, there is no mention of a dwelling there in that period and it is not until the Inquisition post mortem of William Thornhill, in 1499, that we learn of a messuage and seventy acres called 'Knolles'.[181] After that it is possible to trace the families who actually lived there, including the Marshes in the sixteenth century, followed by the Gledhills and Lockwoods.

### The Warren House

The *Warren House* was formerly a public house, situated so close to the boundary between Halifax and Huddersfield that it was sometimes said to lie in Fixby and sometimes in Lindley. It is difficult now to visualise it as a remote moorland inn, but in the early years of the nineteenth century it occupied an isolated position, just below the

*The former* Warren House *in Lindley, now a private dwelling. The name of the inn can still be read on the façade.* Tony Burke

ridge which is the watershed between the two parishes. It was surrounded by the wastes of Lindley Moor. Two major events early in the century were to alter that, dramatically changing the landscape.

The first of these was the Act of 1806 which authorised the building of a new Turnpike Road across the Pennines, from New Hey near Rochdale to Rastrick and Huddersfield. The road was planned to fork on Lindley Moor, to the south of the Warren House, the main branch going directly into Huddersfield, and the northern branch to Rastrick, passing almost alongside the inn. Both branches were given the name New Hey Road. Many of the earlier turnpikes had simply improved the existing highways, but this was a more adventurous project and where new lines of road were to be cut through farmland, any owner who objected was 'desired to meet the trustees at Saville Crowther's... to state the nature of such objection'. Meanwhile the surveyor Mr Brown was to make a valuation and 'produce the same at such meeting'.

In fact, it was at the Warren House that much of the work of the trustees for the new turnpike was carried out: Saville Crowther was the landlord and there were regular meetings there for a number of years, starting in June 1805. The committee's order book not only informs us of the progress made in those years, it actually allows us a glance behind the scenes at the errors, disagreements and misunderstandings that marked the early meetings. Sir John Ramsden, for example, was most unhappy about the section of the road between the 'top of the town' and today's *Junction Inn* (Cowper Pitts as it was then known). His agent wrote to the trustees suggesting that they should not cut out a new line for the road but simply follow the old one, which would 'only want widening and improving in places'. Sir John's letter ended with a veiled threat; 'he cannot', wrote the agent, 'think of submitting... so long as there are any means left for avoiding it'. He was a powerful man but the committee's reply was uncompromising; 'the Road as now set out cannot be varied' they wrote. In a slightly more conciliatory tone, they said they hoped Sir John would not be offended at them for persevering in a plan that would 'be for the public good and of no injury to him'.

There were financial problems, and difficulties with some of the appointed officers, not to mention several false starts. In July 1807, for example, it was 'ordered that a chain be fixed across the Road near Oaks' and then in August it had to 'be removed to Saladin Nook'. Further, there had originally been a plan to site a toll bar at the junction with Blacker Lane, but five months afterwards it was 'ordered that the Foundation... be forthwith removed under the direction of the Committee appointed for the erection thereof'. Eventually, however, despite the mistakes and delays, the road was completed and the toll bars erected. A 'board of the tolls to be taken at Outlane' was 'painted and fixed up on the Bar House' there. The former moorland inn was now close to two new major roads.[182]

The second important event, an *Act of Inclosure*, followed soon afterwards, and it must have transformed the landscape around the Warren House, which was part of Lindley's traditional commons.[183] In 1816 these moorlands were granted to the freeholders, stone walls were built and the new fields given over to farming. Curiously, one of these new 'allotments' provides the clue to the origins of the old house. The major landholder, Thomas Thornhill Esq., received certain of his new enclosures 'in lieu of Rabbit Warren'. It was commonplace in earlier centuries for a gentleman to create a large warren on some part of the heath on his estate, building artificial mounds of soft earth which encouraged the does to burrow and breed. The meat was considered a delicacy and the rabbits had to be protected from poachers, so the original warren house had been built for the keeper high up on Lindley Moor. It is likely that he or a successor sold beer to supplement his income.

# Notes and References

1 Calderdale Archives, West Yorkshire Archive Service (WYAS), Armytage of Kirklees, KM 494.
2 Kirklees Archives, WYAS, Beaumont of Whitley, DD/WBD/VIII/82.
3 Kirklees, WYAS, KC 311/18/1.
4 Kirklees, WYAS, Ramsden of Longley and Byram. DD/RA/f/29/5.
5 Wakefield Registry of Deeds, WYAS, Quarter Sessions Rolls, QS1/68/4.
6 QS1/54/9.
7 QS1/45/5.
8 Quarter Sessions Indictment Books, QS4/23/162.
9 Quarter Sessions Rolls, QS1/55/4.
10 QS1/56/6.
11 QS1/58/6.
12 Quarter Sessions Order Books, QS10/16/31.
13 Quarter Sessions Indictment Books, QS4/30/195.
14 Quarter Sessions Rolls, QS1/57/2.
15 QS1/65/4.
16 QS Box List 21. This was the original reference; it will now have changed.
17 E A H Haigh, ed., *Huddersfield; a most Handsome Town* (Huddersfield, 1992), pp. 65-84.
18 G Head, *A Home Tour through the Manufacturing Districts of England*, (2nd ed. 1968).
19 *Huddersfield Examiner*, 25 May-8 June, 1878.
20 Quarter Sessions Rolls, QS1/68/2.
21 Kirklees, Ramsden, DD/RE. The main surveys and maps are those for 1716, 1778, 1780 and 1797. Rentals cover the years 1798-1854.
22 QS Box List 38. See note 16.
23 Quarter Sessions Indictment Books, QS4/28/178.
24 See note 19.
25 Huddersfield Public Library, Local Studies.
26 Wakefield, WYAS, The papers of Eaton, Smith and Downey, solicitors, C296/226. The clauses relating to pollution were to be an essential part of Ramsden leases in that century.
27 Letter, 3/1/1985 from Norman Burluraux, living in West Germany.
28 Quarter Sessions Indictment Books, QS4/38/286.
29 Kirklees, WYAS, Beaumont, DD/WBD/VIII/10.
30 Kirklees, WYAS, Ramsden, DD/R/dd/I/10.
31 Kirklees, WYAS, Beaumont, DD/WBD/VIII/55.
32 Beaumont, DD/WBE/II/1.
33 Kirklees, WYAS, Ramsden, DD/RE/M.
34 Ramsden, DD/RE/S.
35 Quarter Sessions Indictment Books, QS4/29/146.
36 Kirklees, WYAS, Beaumont, DD/WBM/78.
37 Administration of his goods was granted to his brother in 1651, so he seems to have survived the ordeal.
38 Wakefield Registry of Deeds, WYAS, Eaton, Smith and Downey, C296.
39 C T Clay, 'Yorkshire Deeds', *Yorkshire Archaeological Society, Record Series*, LXV (1924).
40 Kirklees, WYAS, Ramsden, DD/R/dd/1/3
41 Kirklees Archives, WYAS, A map of the Lister Kaye estate in Marsh, 1791.
42 G Redmonds, 'Settlement in Huddersfield before 1800,' *Huddersfield a most Handsome Town*, (1992), pp. 17-36.
43 Kirklees, WYAS, Ramsden, DD/R/dd/IV/3.
44 Borthwick Institute of Historical Research, Wills, vol. 19, fol. 604-5.
45 The spelling of this surname is now usually 'Brook', but 'Brooke' was more common in the past and some families still prefer it.
46 Borthwick Institute of Historical Research, Wills, vol. 14, fol. 115.
47 Kirklees, WYAS, Beaumont, DD/WBD/VIII/24.
48 Beaumont, DD/WBD/VIII/56.
49 Bradford, WYAS, Miscellaneous MSS, A231.
50 C Giles, *Rural Houses of West Yorkshire* (London, 1986), p. 201.
51 E J Law, 'An Exemplary Barn', *Old West Riding*, Vol. 4, part 2, pp. 31-32.
52 Kirklees, WYAS, Beaumont, DD/WBD/VIII/17.
53 Beaumont, DD/WBD/II/44.
54 Wakefield Registry of Deeds, WYAS, Quarter Sessions Rolls, QS1/51/4.
55 C T Clay, 'Yorkshire Deeds', *Yorkshire Archaeological Society, Record Series*, LXXVI (1930), p. 120.
56 *Ibid.*, p. 119.
57 Claremont, Leeds, WYAS, Clarke Thornhill, DD12/II.
58 Two documents survive with details of this enclosure, one in the Whitley Beaumont papers; DD/WBE/II/1, and one in an account book of the Ramsden family; DD/RL/f/4a.
59 'Notebook of Captain John Pickering', *Thoresby Society*, XI, pp. 99-100.
60 G Redmonds, ed., *Yorkshire Deeds in Kansas* (Huddersfield, 1999), MS Q21/D5.
61 Kirklees, WYAS, Beaumont, WBR/2.
62 Kirklees, WYAS, Ahier MSS.
63 Quarter Sessions Rolls, QS1/45/6.

64 Kirklees, WYAS, Ramsden, DD/RE/S.
65 *Ibid.*, DD/RE/R.
66 There are interesting documents relating to the Whitacres' Huddersfield estates in Wakefield Registry of Deeds, WYAS, Eaton, Smith and Downey, C296/231.
67 Kirklees, WYAS, Ramsden, DD/RE/R.
68 Nottinghamshire County Record Office, Savile papers, DD SR.
69 Bradford, WYAS, Spencer Stanhope, 4/11/70/2.
70 Kirklees, WYAS, Ramsden, DD/R/dd/IV/2.
71 Ramsden, DD/R/dd/IV/12.
72 Quarter Sessions Indictment Books, QS4/3/212.
73 C M Fraser and K Emsley, eds, 'The Court Rolls of the Manor of Wakefield 1639-40', *The Wakefield Court Rolls Series*, 1, pp. 102-03.
74 Quarter Sessions Indictment Books, QS4/25.
75 *Ibid.*, QS4/4.
76 Quarter Sessions Rolls, QS1/45/9.
77 Quarter Sessions Indictment Books, QS4/36.
78 'Deed endorsed "Bridge Royd", 1236-58', *Yorkshire Archaeological and Topographical Journal*, IX (1886), p. 393.
79 Quarter Sessions Rolls, QS1/95/4.
80 Kirklees, WYAS, KC174/3/1.
81 G Redmonds, *Old Huddersfield 1500-1800* (Huddersfield, 1981), pp. 41-42.
82 Quarter Sessions Order Books, QS10/2.
83 Kirklees, WYAS, Ramsden DD/R/dd/IV/1.
84 Calderdale Archives, WYAS, Armytage of Kirklees KM177.
85 J Lister, ed., 'West Riding Sessions Rolls 1597-1602', *The Yorkshire Archaeological and Topographical Association, Record Series*, III (1888), pp. 38-39.
86 Quarter Sessions Rolls, QS1/60/4.
87 In the past a 'hamlet' was a sub-division of a township with some degree of autonomy.
88 M A Faull and S A Moorhouse, *West Yorkshire: an Archaeological Survey to AD 1500*, 2 (Wakefield, 1981), p. 408.
89 'Subsidy Roll for Agbrigg and Morley', *Yorkshire Archaeological and Topographical Journal*, II (1872), p. 51.
90 C T Clay, 'Bradley, a Grange of Fountains', *Yorkshire Archaeological Journal*, XXIX (1929), pp. 97-106.
91 W T Lancaster, ed., *Fountains Chartulary*, 2 vols (Leeds, 1915).
92 I would like to acknowledge here the work done by Michael B. Fisk on the history of the families at Bradley Hall: I have benefited much from his letters and transcripts of inventories over the years.
93 J S Purvis, 'Select XVI Century Causes in Tithe', *Yorkshire Archaeological Society*, Record Series, CXIV (1949).
94 D Whomsley, 'William Ramsden of Longley, Gentleman, 1514-1580, Agent in Monastic Property', *Yorkshire Archaeological Journal*, XLII , part 166 (1968).
95 G Redmonds, 'Halifax and District', *Yorkshire Surnames Series*, Part 3 (Huddersfield, 2002).
96 Kirklees, WYAS, Plan of an Estate in the Town of Huddersfield, late the property of Sir Thomas Pilkington, Bt, deceased, as divided into lots for sale, 1829.
97 G Redmonds, 'Colne Bridge Forge', *The Heirs of Woodsome* (Huddersfield, 1982), pp. 36-47.
98 Kirklees, WYAS, Heaton Manor court rolls, WBR/II/11.
99 Kirklees, WYAS, Beaumont, DD/WBE/152.
100 Bradford, WYAS, Spencer Stanhope Papers, (Colnebridge Forge accounts).
101 Kirklees, WYAS, Beaumont, DD/WBE/1/5-141,
102 Beaumont, DD/WBE/ 151 and 152.
103 Beaumont, DD/WBE/152.
104 Beaumont, DD/WBE/98.
105 Beaumont, DD/WBD/III/223.
106 Beaumont, DD/WBC/166.
107 Beaumont, DD/WBC/218.
108 A J Brooke, 'Jacobinism and Unrest in the Huddersfield Area, 1799-1803', *Old West Riding*, Vol. 2, part 1, p. 24.
109 Kirklees, WYAS, Beaumont, DD/WBC/177.
110 Wakefield Registry of Deeds, WYAS, Land Tax for Fartown and Kirkheaton, QE/13.
111 Wakefield, WYAS, Eaton, Smith and Downey, Solicitors, C296/113.
112 G W Tomlinson, 'The Proposed Tower on Castle Hill', *The Yorkshire Archaeological Journal*, XIV (London, 1898), pp. 515-56
113 W J Varley, *Castle Hill: Almondbury* (Huddersfield, 1973).
114 C A Hulbert, *Annals of the Church and Parish of Almondbury* (London, 1882), p. 11.
115 There are several archive copies of this important document, e.g. MS 205 Claremont, Leeds. A transcript is in the local history section of Huddersfield Library.
116 G Redmonds, *Almondbury: Places and Place-Names* (Huddersfield, 1983), pp. 15-16.
117 J Nicholson, *Old Yorkshire*, New Series 1, pp. 19-36.
118 Wakefield, WYAS, Quarter Sessions Order Books, QS10.
119 Quarter Sessions Rolls, QSI/24/10.
120 J E Taylor, *Historic Almondbury* (Huddersfield, 1977), p. 9.
121 This map will be referred to several times. The original is now back in Huddersfield Library, but several copies of varying quality exist.
122 G Redmonds, ed., *Yorkshire Deeds in Kansas* (Huddersfield, 1999), HUD 117.
123 'Longley Old Hall', Yorkshire Vernacular Buildings Study Group, No. 29, p. 58.

124 Kirklees, WYAS, The accounts of William Ramsden, woodward general, 1544-45, DD/RL/f/4a.

125 Kirklees, Ramsden, DD/R/dd/V/29.

126 F Collins, 'Index to the Yorkshire Wills in the time of the Commonwealth', Yorkshire Archaeological Society, Record Series, I (1885).

127 *Ibid.*, p.133.

128 Quarter Sessions Order books, QS10/19.

129 G S Phillips, *Walks Round Huddersfield* (Huddersfield, 1848, reprinted 1987), p. 20.

130 Green-Armytage deeds, in the family's possession.

131 G Redmonds, 'Huddersfield and District', *Yorkshire Surnames Series* Part 2, (1992).

132 H Taylor, ed., 'The Parish Register of Almondbury 1557-1598', *Yorkshire Archaeological Society, Parish Register Section*, CXXXIX (1974).

133 G Redmonds, *Almondbury: Places and Place-Names* (Huddersfield, 1983), pp. 55-56.

134 Rev. T Lewthwaite, 'Sketches of Newsome', *Home Words, Newsome Parish Magazine*, 1882-86.

135 Kirklees, WYAS, J W Wilson and Son, tinsmiths, Lockwood, B/JWW.

136 H J Morehouse, *The History and Topography of the Parish of Kirkburton and of the Graveship of Holme* (Huddersfield, 1861), pp. 228-241.

137 G Redmonds, *Old Huddersfield: 1500-1800* (Huddersfield, 1981), pp. 42-45.

138 Borthwick Institute of Historical Research, Wills, vol. 11, fol. 273.

139 Kirklees, WYAS, Dalton Manor court roll 1483, M/D.

140 Claremont, WYAS, Wakefield Manor court rolls, MD 225/1/180.

141 *Ibid.*, MD 225/1/190.

142 *Ibid.*, MD 225/1/216.

143 'Testamenta Eboracensia', *Surtees Society*, XLV (1865), p. 356.

144 Kirklees, WYAS, Dalton Manor court roll 1556, M/D.

145 *Ibid.*, 1526.

146 Kirklees, WYAS, Ramsden, DD/R/dd/I/19.

147 Ramsden, WYAS, DD/R/dd/I/20.

148 *Ibid.*, DD/R/dd/V/9

149 G Redmonds, ed., *Yorkshire Deeds in Kansas* (Huddersfield, 1999), HUD 12.

150 Kirklees, WYAS, Kidd Mellor deeds, KC6.

151 Claremont, WYAS, MD211.

152 Kirklees, Beaumont, DD/WBE/11.

153 Claremont, WYAS, Wakefield Manor court rolls, MD 225/1/212.

154 Wakefield Registry of Deeds, WYAS, Quarter Sessions Indictment Books, QS4/23/119.

155 Claremont, WYAS, Wakefield court rolls, MD 225/1/199

156 L Tolson, *History and Annals of Kirkheaton* (Kendal, 1929).

157 E.g. A S Ellis, ed., 'Dodsworth's Yorkshire Notes', *Yorkshire Archaeological Journal*, VII (1882), p. 414.

158 'Wills in the York Registry', *Yorkshire Archaeological Society Record Series*, XXXII (1902), p. 21.

159 Kirklees, WYAS, Beaumont, DD/WBD/VIII/73.

160 Quarter Sessions Indictment Books, QS4/33/202

161 Quarter Sessions Order Books, QS10/2/102.

162 T Langdale, *A Topographical Dictionary of Yorkshire* (Ripon 1822).

163 Kirklees, WYAS, Thornhill, T/S/a/37.

164 Thornhill, T/S/b/9.

165 W B Crump and G Ghorbal, *History of the Huddersfield Woollen Industry* (reprinted, Huddersfield, 1967), p. 39.

166 Calderdale Archives, WYAS, Armytage of Kirklees, KM/352.

167 Kirklees, WYAS, formerly Folio Pamphlets.

168 G Redmonds, *Slaithwaite: Places and Place-names* (Huddersfield, 1988), p.17.

169 G Fellows Jensen, *Scandinavian Settlement Names in Yorkshire* (Copenhagen, 1972), pp. 5-12.

170 M L Faull and S A Moorhouse, eds, *West Yorkshire: an Archaeological Survey to AD 1500*, 2 (Wakefield, 1981), p.374.

171 W P Baildon, ed., 'Court Rolls of the Manor of Wakefield, 1297-1309', *Yorkshire Archaeological Society, Record Series*, XXXVI (1906).

172 Claremont, WYAS, Clarke Thornhill, DD/12/II/3.

173 Kirklees, Beaumont, DD/WBD/X/26.

174 Kirklees, Almondbury Court Rolls, DD/R/M.

175 J Horsfall Turner, ed., *The Rev. Oliver Heywood, B.A., 1630-1702; his autobiography, diaries, anecdote and event books*, 2 (Brighouse 1881-85), p.256.

176 J Charlesworth, ed., 'Wakefield Manor Book 1709', *Yorkshire Archaeological Society Record Series*, CI (1939).

177 Claremont, WYAS, Clarke Thornhill, DD/12/II/3.

178 C T Clay, ed., 'Yorkshire Deeds', *Yorkshire Archaeological Society, Record Series*, LXV (1924), p. 51.

179 *Ibid.*, p. 58.

180 Claremont, WYAS, Wakefield Court Rolls, MD 225/1/163/1 and MD 225/1431, m. 3d.

181 *Calendar of Inquisitions post mortem, Henry VII*, 1 (London, 1898).

182 Wakefield, WYAS, Turnpike Trusts, RT41.

183 Kirklees, WYAS, Official and Administrative Records, E/H.

# $\mathcal{I}$NDEX